Railroads in the Woods

PUBLISHED BY
Oso Publishing Company
31328 North Brooks Creek Road
Arlington, Washington 98223

Library of Congress Cataloging-in-Publication Data
Labbe, John T.
        Railroads in the Woods / by John T. Labbe and Vernon Goe.
            p. cm.
        Originally published: Berkley, Calif. : Howell-North, 1961.
        Includes index.
        ISBN 0-9647521-0-7
        1. Logging railroads--United States. I. Goe, Vernon. II. Title.
        TF23.L38 1995
        385'.54'0973--dc20   95-52314
                                                                           CIP

Printed and bound in the United States of America.

Railroads in the Woods

John T. Labbe
Vernon Goe

Oso
Publishing
COMPANY
Washington State • United States of America • 1995

Contents

Opposite: No.1 of the Carlton and Coast Railroad drifts lazily down grade beside the North Fork of the Yamhill River. She was No. 6256 from the Baldwin Works in 1882, and she has been around. She served on the lines of the Oregon Railway and Navigation Company for many years, and under many different numbers, before the Carlton Lumber Company bought her for the Carlton and Coast in early 1910. The little woodburning Mogul put in another 15 years in the woods before Flora Logging Company scrapped her in the late 1920's.

Weister photo from the University of Oregon Library

End Papers: Weyerhauser's spectacular Baird's Creek bridge in Cowlitz County, on the line out of Longview. This bridge is 1,130 feet long and 235 feet high and still in service.

Kenneth S. Brown photo from West Coast Lumberman's Association

Above: As it was in the beginning. The timber grew to the water's edge all along the western slope of the Cascades and the early logger had to but tip the trees into the water and float them to market.

University of Oregon Collection.

Acknowledgements

Several years ago the authors decided that an effort should be made to seek out and preserve old logging photographs of historical interest. The old-timers who had acquired them originally were nearing the end of the road, and too often, the families failed to realize their value. As it was, we were pretty late in our quest. Many fine collections were burned or thrown away before we arrived. But the many others that we were able to save were more than worth our efforts.

The search for old-timers and their families carried us all the way from tumbled-down shacks in the deep woods to mansions in the cities. It carried us many thousands of miles over many weekends. It was a fascinating experience that brought us hordes of new friends. Almost without exception, these people who had never seen us before felt such sympathy for our project that they pressed their pictures on us, and before we left they made sure that we had the names of all the friends who might be helpful. Out of this tremendous interest was born the idea for this book.

Not everyone we met had pictures, but all were quick to help us with their reminiscences which often unraveled the tangled skein of history or gave us a lead to new sources. Inevitably we received far more pictures than could be incorporated in any single book, but whether we were able to use them here or not, we are eternally grateful to have received them. In some instances we found several prints of the same picture, in which case we chose the one from which we obtained the best reproduction.

The list of those whose pictures appear within these pages should bring memories to many who will read it. No one could have worked in the woods along the Columbia without knowing of them personally, or by reputation; and though many pictures have come from sons and daughters, the names will bring recollections of other days. To each of them we express our thanks and the hope that this book will live up to their expectations. There are Jens Lerback and Fred Hendrickson, Mrs. McPherson, Fred Seal, Hi Davis, Bill Soderberg, Arthur Clarkson, Mr. Nordlund, W. W. Brock, Sam Sonneland, Cy Vaughn, Mrs. Burns, Henry Mooers, E. W. Anderson, H. S. Turley, Tom Timony, Willard Evenson, George Witham, R. S. Lindsay, Roy McCourry, Rudy Larson, J. G. Kilner, H. C. Swenson, Eber Brown, Cecil Davis and his son Cecil, Jr., Babe Britton, Mr. Richardson, Mark Elliot, Mr. Duggan, Charles Wirkkala, Mrs. Cora Yandell, J. H. McMilan, Colvin's Tavern in Clatskanie, Norman Elsner, Willis Gulker, Mrs. Kelty, George Morrice, J. T. Buckley, Mrs. J. F. Blair, Ed Peterson, Ray Davis, M. E. Whitbeck, E. P. Stamm, Charlie Smith, Mr. Park, Ben Stark, Joe Schrieber, Clyde Lowe, Ernest Strom, Art Johnson, M. C. Barhan, Cecil Bryant, Ernie Splester, A. H. Sliffe, C. F. Colvin, Frank Barrett, Oscar Lindberg, William Beegle, Mrs. Beeker and Mrs. Albert Nelson.

In addition to the old-timers, there was another group that contributed much in the way of information and valuable photographs. These were people who shared our interest in collecting old photographs and recording history. The list is a long one, but each one of them went out of his way to dig up the pictures we needed and helped us untangle some aspect of history. Many hours of patient correspondence is represented here, and it has truly been a pleasure to have worked with them. There are J. M. McClelland, Jr., of the Longview Daily News, James Brady of the M. F. Brady Equipment Company, B. H. Ward, David L. Stearns, John and George Powers, D. S. Richter, Gregory Kamholz, George B. Abdill, W. B. Fowler, Robert Chamberlain, C. W. Mendenhall, S. B. Lawrence, Lamar Ferguson, Walter R. Grande, L. Harrison, Thomas T. Taber, Richard Buike, F. Hal Higgins, Jack Holst, Albert Farrow, H. J. Vanderveen, Randolph Brandt, Kramer Adams and John S. Anderson.

We are most grateful for the fine cooperation we received from many institutions and organizations in the Northwest. Mrs. Nancy Hacker, of the Oregon Historical Society, helped us to turn up many fine prints. Mrs. Inez Fortt guided us through the hundreds of negatives in the Oregon Collections of the University of Oregon Library. We received much help from the Seattle Historical Society, the Wahkiakum County Museum at Cathlamet, the West Coast Lumbermen's Association, the Spokane, Portland and Seattle Railway's "Dope Bucket," Miller-Freeman Publications and Weyerhaeuser Company.

Above all, we owe a debt of gratitude to Ed Colvin whose fine work with copy camera and darkroom is largely responsible for the high quality of the photographs appearing here. Many of these pictures were literally brought back from oblivion through the application of difficult photographic techniques. Nor can we overlook Joe Perelle who stepped into the breach when Ed was not available and did an equally fine job. It was they who made our dreams for this book come true.

Introduction

The era of the logging railroad was synonymous with the great era of logging. Each was dependent on the other. The versatility of the railroad made it possible to tap the most inaccessible tract of timber with high production equipment and methods. Only the railroad could carry away the logs as fast as the loggers could supply them.

The logging railroad was a thing apart. Beyond making use of a locomotive to haul cars with flanged wheels along steel rails it bore little resemblance to the common conception of railroading. It was a highly specialized operation requiring specially developed equipment; and it was manned by a special breed of men. They came out of the deep woods of the Northwest, of Michigan and Wisconsin, or the Scandinavian countries, to write a thrilling chapter in the history of the iron horse. And when the job was done they picked up the axe and the saw and returned to the woods.

The logging railroad was made up of light rail tacked to flimsy ties and laid on scanty ballast. It had grades of six, or eight, or ten per cent, up which it worried the monstrous logging machines with the aid of geared engines. And having set these machines in production, unending trains of logs were dropped down the grades on hand brakes. It handled cars of logs eighty feet long, snaking them around thirty degree curves on disconnected trucks. It carried many trains operating on a single track, and often without the aid of dispatching.

The men were not bound by railroad tradition or experience. They made their own rules, established their own methods and created their own equipment. They knew but one driving force—the challenge of the growing timber just beyond the cuttings. No job was ever impossible. There was always a way to get the next tree—and the next, and the next. It was only a case of developing the right technique for accomplishing it.

It was a hard and dangerous life, but it was also a happy, lusty one. The men griped about their jobs, about the living conditions, about the cooks; they cussed bosses, each other and themselves. They quit at the drop of a hat to take other jobs equally bad, and they came back to the first job only to quit again. But none sought work outside the woods as long as it was available. And now that it is no more, a picture or an anecdote can bring a quick tear of nostalgia and a sigh for the good old days.

The panorama of railroad logging was made up of many scenes peculiarly its own. It was a little tank engine hustling the crew car up the mountain in the early dawn, the steam from its stack joining the swirling mists in the dark tree tops. It was brakies hunched against the rain as they rode the sets of empty disconnects that snaked along behind the churning Shay. It was the lonesome call of the steam whistle echoing through the aisles of silent trees. It was brakies running along the long loads of swaying logs as they set the brakes with their hickeys. It was the writhing contortions of abandoned trackage laid bare along the denuded hills. It was cars going up and down the steep side of a mountain on a cable that creaked and sang as it felt the tug of the distant donkey engine. It was bounding deer that raced ahead of the pilot before springing lightly into a thicket. It was spindly trestles over roaring trout streams. Too, it was runaways and spilled loads and soft tracks. It was fallen trees and sliding hills and broken bridges. Careless men died easily.

But in the final analysis it was more than all this. The logging railroad was the outstanding characteristic of the great days of logging. It is the symbol that marks an era—an era that can never come again.

John T. Labbe
Vernon Goe
Portland, Oregon
1961

The Beginning

When the first settlers came seeking homes in the western wilderness their great need was for housing. Those who came into the Oregon Country found the raw materials in unbelievable abundance. Mighty forests covered the land from tidewater to the snow covered peaks of the Cascade Range.

The waterways that threaded this dark and fertile land provided the first avenues of commerce. Along the banks grew the settlements and trading posts. Docks were built to welcome the ships in from the sea, and mills were built to grind the grain and saw the logs from this new country.

The same rivers and streams that provided communication were ideal for transporting logs to the mills. Loggers working for the lumber companies, and settlers clearing their claims, found it convenient to work their logs into the water where they could be floated to market.

As the new settlements grew they pushed further inland from the water's edge and it became necessary to drag the logs to the water from ever increasing distances. By the 1870's bull teams had become the accepted method of logging. Six or seven teams of slogging oxen would be hitched to a turn of logs. The logs were dragged over a road built up of cross skids made from poles, and the poles were greased to make the logs slide more readily. Usually the ends of the logs were sniped to prevent them from hanging up, and oftentimes they were peeled. Later, as the skidroads became longer, horses replaced the slow moving oxen on many jobs.

In the 1880's steam came to the woods, and the industrial revolution had caught up with the logger. The steam boiler was harnessed to a winch and a steel cable took over the job of dragging the logs from the faithful bulls. The potential of this new power was enormous and the logger was quick to realize it. Within a few short years new production methods had changed the entire logging scene.

By the 1880's, in fact, the entire West was coming of age. The great era of the railroads was at hand and East and West were being tied together by the ribbons of steel. So it was not surprising that the more progressive loggers should begin to think in terms of railroads to handle this rapidly expanding production between the woods and the river.

The early railroads were just a step away from the bull teams. They began at the river bank, where the bulls had dumped their logs, and they ran back a mile or two to the logging site. And because transportation of the equipment into these out of the way places was difficult, it usually consisted of light tank engines and small cars or trucks. The spar tree was still in the future, and a carload was still comprised of what could be rolled on from a rollway. But the logger was learning fast and the steam winch that was helping the bull teams out on the skidroad was soon helping the loaders to roll the logs onto the cars, and to pile them higher and higher.

With the coming of the mainline railroads the lumber companies were no longer confined to the rivers, for the railroad now offered an equally attractive means of receiving the raw materials and shipping the finished product. Whole new regions tributary to the rails were now available to the logger. But in order to take advantage of this new field of operations it was necessary to make use of a railroad of his own, connecting with the mainline and ultimately with his market. The logger who was thus situated had little difficulty in transporting his materials and supplies to his operation, and was able to make use of heavier equipment. Oftentimes he acquired discarded locomotives from the mainline, and if his logs were to be shipped over the line, he used regular equipment supplied him by the railroad.

The success of the railroad was such that it soon became accepted practice. The smaller operators were forced by the competition to imitate their larger competitors. As is always the case, this placed a serious burden on the shoulders of the small operator. But loggers, over the years, have been a versatile and imaginative group, seldom inclined to be led by common practice. Thus, in the interests of economy and dire necessity many strange and wonderful contraptions made their appearance in the woods. And, crude and clumsy though they may have appeared, they usually got the job done.

Below: An early logging scene in the hills east of Portland. Before the advent of machinery, these loggers are getting out some beautiful timber with the aid of bull teams.

Fred Seal

Above: Timber along the lower Columbia River grew thickly on the ground. Here the fallers for the Peninsula Lumber Company, at Columbia City, pose on their springboards. These boards fitted into a notch cut into the stump of the tree, raising the fallers above the brush and making it possible to cut the tree where the trunk was smaller in diameter. Sometimes these men worked many feet above the ground, working their way up from one board to another, and, in fact, some of the earliest spar trees were climbed in this way.

Labbe and Goe

Right: This log chute was located on the Yaquina River, near Elk City, Oregon. It is typical of the chutes used extensively throughout the logging region.

Oregon Historical Society

Left: Booming logs that have been skidded into the water along the banks of the Columbia River. End of the skidroad can be seen in the lower left corner of the photo.

Jens Lerback and Fred Hendrickson

Below: Kelly Logging Company bull teams at Stringtown, a community that has since disappeared. It was located on the lower Columbia River just east of Big Creek and not far from Knappa, Oregon.

Mrs. McPherson

Above: Bull teams of the Bridal Veil Lumbering Company bring their logs to the landing above the mill at Palmer, Oregon. From here to the mill they will be handled by the railroad.

D. L. Stearns

Right: One reason they welcomed the logging railroad in the Astoria area. This 14 footer was brought out by C. C. Masten, at Svensen. They even had to block it out of the brush with the donkey, judging by the rigging on it.

Bill Soderberg

Above: A very early adaptation of the steam winch to use in the woods. The steam boiler is permanently mounted over a dutch oven and the winch drums are located in a separate installation. The winch has taken over the yarding job from the bulls, but has not yet been adapted for loading. This was an early Robert Dollar operation at Usal on the northern California coast.

Miller-Freeman Publications

Above: Very early steam donkey used by the Bridal Veil Lumbering Company. This was the original design of the Dolbeer donkey which is often considered to be the original donkey engine. Note the line tender whose job it was to coil the line as it was brought in by the little gypsy drum.

D. L. Stearns

Below: This was Brock's camp at Eufaula just down river from Longview, Washington, as it looked about 1897. The bulls have brought the logs to the landing in the foreground where they are rolled aboard the cars for the trip to the river. The Rattler is handling the train, while the little Ant is held in standby—up beyond the corral. Building at the far right is the schoolhouse.

C. Kinsey photo from Hi Davis

Top: A scene on the Benson Logging and Lumbering Company operation at Oak Point, on the Washington side of the Columbia. They did things the hard way in those days. The logs were rolled onto the cars by hand with the aid of a crank jack, such as the one held by the third man from the left.

H. G. Nelson photo-From Arthur Clarkson

Middle: Loading railroad cars from rollways. No spar trees are in evidence, as yet, but the loggers are using a block and line to take the place of the peavey and the jack. Scene is the camp of Charlie Masten, near Svensen, Oregon.

Nelson photo courtesy Mr. Nordlund

Bottom: First railroad show on the Columbia River. Scene on B. F. Brock's Mosquito and Coal Creek Railroad at Eufaula, Washington. Logs are rolled onto the cars from the rollway. Note the arrangement of "outriggers" designed to keep the little trucks from upsetting while being loaded. Gauge of the line was 3 feet, and the trains were backed down to the dump to avoid the possibility of damage to the lokey. The engine is the "Ant," which went to work here in October 1883.

Cawthorn photo from W. W. Brock

Right: Early tank engine at work on Vancouver Island.

B. H. Ward

Below: A couple of early loggers strike a "classic" pose in front of Louis Saldern's little Porter tank engine near Grays River, Washington. Porter #812 was turned out in February of 1887 and opened rail operations on the lower Columbia River when Trullinger acquired her for his operation just east of Astoria, Oregon. Saldern later used the engine on an operation near Clatskanie, Oregon, before moving to the Washington side of the river in the spring of 1899.

Sam Sonneland

Above: A dismantled steam donkey heads for the woods through the streets of Forest Grove, Oregon. The muddy city streets are probably the best going the horses will find between here and the woods, but by the time the leaves begin to show on the trees the logs will be headed for market. Whole railroads reached the woods in the same way.

Hi Davis

Left: A pleasant interlude. This little engine was handling log trains for Yeon and Pelton near Rainier, Oregon when it wasn't providing a backdrop for the pretty girls.

Opposite top: A little engine on the Ft. Bragg Railroad in northern California with some big Redwood logs. This little 2-4-2 tank engine was built by Baldwin in 1886. She was No. 1 on the Ft. Bragg.

B. H. Ward

Below: Early log train of Sommerville Brothers near Napavine, Washington. The locomotive was first acquired by Simon Benson for his original operation at Oak Point on the Columbia river. The fellow sitting on the stump is "Roaring Ed" Baker, later superintendent of Long-Bell's Ryderwood operation. He has hold of a peavey, which probably represents the sum total of equipment for loading and unloading the cars-and is probably why they aren't piled higher. Judging by the "light" on the rear of the engine, they get caught after dark now and then.

J. M. McClelland, Jr.

Above: Small logging show of J. B. Miller Logging Company near Ollalie Slough, not far from Toledo, Oregon. Logs were handled to the dump by the little loco and a set of trucks. The engine was a former steam dummy from the Independence & Monmouth Railway at Independence, Oregon.

Hi Davis

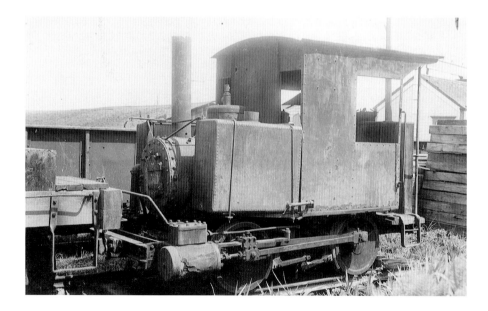

Left: A tiny lokey from the Big Tree Country. This was Holmes Eureka Lumber Company No. 1, of Eureka, California, in the heart of the redwoods. She reposes here in a Eureka scrap yard after many years of service in the woods.

Bert Ward

Above: An early landing on K-M Mountain in 1901. This was on the Saldern Logging Company show near Grays River, Washington.
J. F. Ford from J. M. McClelland, Jr.

Below: The Star Logging and Lumbering Company's No. 4 was a 42-inch gauge engine from Portland's street car lines. This operation near Rainier, Oregon was later taken over by Yeon and Pelton.
Mrs. Burns

Top: No. 1 of the Silverton Lumber Company is busily engaged with a work train during construction days at the turn of the century near Silverton, Oregon.

Drake photo from Oregon Historical Society

Middle: Scene on the Seaside Spruce Lumber Company line. Mooers, who logged for Sorenson and later had their own operation at Skamokawa, also logged here at Seaside, Oregon.

Henry Mooers

Bottom: The J. B. Miller dump on Ollalie Slough, near Toledo, Oregon. The engine had an 0-4-2 wheel arrangement, and began life as a steam dummy.

Hi Davis

Above: A beautiful example of an early mainline locomotive adapted for use in the woods. Note also that the mainline is supplying the cars. This was the Coal Creek Logging and Timber Company of Cosmopolis, Washington. The railroad operation, however, was in the vicinity of Montesano. This type of logging railroad required a more substantial roadbed and track, but savings in equipment and handling usually offset the higher cost.

Cy Vaughn

Right: Porter tank engine used by Saldern Logging Company on K-M Mountain, near Grays River, in 1901. Engineer Winters poses on his engine between his companions, Dietrich and Black.

J. M. McClelland, Jr.

Above: Bulls bring a turn into the dump on Discovery Bay, not far from Port Townsend, Washington. The three logs contain 12,750 feet, which is a good load for six yoke of oxen. Millions of feet of fine timber was rafted along the beaches of Puget Sound in the early days. *J. H. Le Ballister photo, C. F. Colvin*

Right: Loading a big log with jacks in the early years of the Deep River Logging Company. Disconnected trucks could be coupled closely to accommodate such short cuts. The fellow with the right-hand jack is Gus Magneson, who still lives and works not far from Deep River. *J. F. Ford photo from Frank Barrett*

Below: Horse logging on the Olympic Peninsula at Leland, not far from Hood Canal. Those three fine logs have just been par-buckled aboard the car with horses and line. *C. F. Colvin*

Above: The Oregon and Southeastern was a common carrier operating out of Cottage Grove, Oregon. Through most of its existence its fortunes have been closely tied to the lumber industry. Today, as the Oregon, Pacific and Eastern, it is under Georgia-Pacific control. Mogul No. 3 was once No. 16, "Ophir," on the Virginia and Truckee Railroad, and it came to the O&SE by way of the Union Pacific, OR&N and the Salem, Falls City and Western. The 4-spot started out with the Oregon Pacific and the Corvallis and Eastern before ending up on the O&SE roster. *B. H. Ward*

Below: This little dummy worked along Beaver Creek above Clatskanie, Oregon. The Oregon Lumber Company had a sawmill at Beaver Falls kept busy by the little engine and a set of trucks. This was but one of many mills in Oregon and Washington operated by the Eccles interests of Salt Lake City, most of which were known locally as the "Mormon mills." The engine was brought down the river after her stint on the street railways in Utah. *Oscar Lindberg*

Above: Thought to be the first Shay on Puget Sound, Mosher & McDonald's No. 1 was No. 337 from the Lima works. Built in March of 1891, it is pictured here the following June, hard at work in the woods. She was named "Belle," and the name was painted under the cab window. And isn't that horseshoe on the headlight upside down?
Seattle Historical Society

Left: Very early view of the Benson dump at Clatskanie. The little Shay has brought down a log to be sent to the St. Louis World Fair. Benson finished up his operations out of Oak Point on the Washington side of the Columbia River and moved across to Clatskanie on the Oregon side in 1902.
E. W. Anderson

Above: Homemade pole road engine working for the Chan Wilson sawmill at Hudson, just back of Rainier, Oregon, about 1906.

Tom Timony

Right: Near Johnson's Mill, Coquille River, Oregon, a small locomotive of original design lets its load down to the river along a flimsy wooden trestle. The engine was probably built up from the remains of an early donkey engine.

Ernest A. Stauff—courtesy Miller-Freeman Publications

Bridges and Trestles

With timber growing in profusion everywhere near Kelso, Washington, the early logger could pick and choose. Once he was free to leave the river banks the whole vast area was available to him. And it is interesting to note that his first consideration was for quality. If the terrain offered problems that made railroading appear all but impossible he was not impressed. His ingenuity was equal to the challenge.

No location was too remote for him to get in with his equipment, and once installed there was always some way to get the logs out. In the beginning the log chute was a common device. Some of these were a mile or more in length, but they were hard on timber and the smoking logs were a potential fire hazard. Soon the railroads were making use of the switchback to make the descent to the water; and ultimately the incline solved the problem of precipitous hillsides. The incline was simply a railroad laid straight up the side of a mountain by which cars and locomotives went up and down at the end of a wire rope controlled by a donkey engine.

Gullies and canyons proved no problem. The loggers just filled them up with logs and laid their rails across. Some of the deeper ones required some spectacular cribbing that gobbled up thousands of feet of prime logs, but there was no other way. As the timber receded it increased in value to the point where this practice was no longer economical and the logger turned to the pile driver. And now their log trains moved from ridge to ridge across these spidery trestles.

As the rails worked further back into the mountains the problems became more severe. Grades increased from four or five per cent to as much as 15 per cent in places. Canyons grew deeper and wider, requiring more and more spectacular bridges. Grading became heavier, with now and then a tunnel required. Inclines were added above inclines. And finally, to stay close to the working area, whole camps were mounted on flanged wheels and moved deep into the woods.

Opposite: A little Yeon and Pelton engine feels its way through heavy timber near Delena, not far from Rainier, Oregon.

J. F. Ford from John Yeon's album, courtesy J. Brady

Below: A single tree makes a train load for Ostrander's 2-spot. Each log was 30 feet long and scaled about 11,000 board feet. Logs like these would be worth a small fortune today, but when they were logged they brought about $300 apiece.

J. M. McClelland, Jr.

Above: This switchback on the Benson Logging and Lumbering Company operation, at Clatskanie, Oregon is typical of early tracklaying. The lower leg follows up the bed of the creek on a low trestle, and the upper leg scrambles up the side of a hill with as little excavating as possible. The upper leg was said to be a grade of 14 per cent. Barely visible at the top of the hill is a Shay.

Miller-Freeman Publications

Above: Peterson's log chute, below Rainier, Oregon. The head of the chute can be seen at the extreme left where a donkey is located to drag the logs from the dump to the head of the chute. The logs were then sent down the chute to the slough far below. This was the operation taken over by Yeon and Pelton in the fall of 1901, when the chute was replaced by the first incline used in the woods. The steam dummy is one of those used by Yeon and Pelton for many years, here still decked out in the elaborate coach superstructure.

Oregon Historical Society

Right: About all it took to keep an early logging operation going was a good blacksmith, a strong helper and a boy to work the bellows. This is the crew that performed the job for Yeon and Pelton. The man in the beard was Ed Carreau, a blacksmith and machinist of rare talent, although totally illiterate. His genius kept the operation at a constant peak of high efficiency.

J. F. Ford photo from Jim Brady

Above: Smith Powers No. 7 working a switchback near Powers, Oregon, in Coos County. Smith Powers trackage was all built up on low trestlework in the woods.

John and George Powers

Left: Against a background of beautiful big trees, a little Shay of the Oak Point Piling and Timber Company moves out another train of fine logs. Oak Point, Washington, in 1907.

E. W. Anderson

Above: Yeon and Pelton incline below Rainier, Oregon. The incline was 3200 feet long and varied from 5 per cent to 33 per cent grade.

J. F. Ford photo from John Yeon's album, courtesy J. Brady

Above: When this bridge was built, timber was cheap-and so was labor. Loco is the Yeon and Pelton No. 5, a 42" gauge Climax and the newest engine on this busy line near Rainier, Oregon. Behind the engine is a car mounted donkey engine, operated on steam borrowed from the locomotive boiler. Date is 1908.

George Witham

Left: Log bridge on the Columbia and Nehalem Valley Railroad, which was incorporated in January of 1900. The line never got very far from the Columbia River. Deer Island Logging Company came along later and made use of part of the right of way.

Photo from Mrs. Burns

Above: Deep River Logging Company's Shay No. 5 crosses a cribbed bridge. The country around Deep River, Washington, is plenty rough, and the easiest way to cross a canyon was to fill it up with logs. While this picture was taken near the turn of the century, the last trains didn't come rumbling down the line until 1955.

Willard Evenson

Right: A bridge on the Columbia and Nehalem Valley Railroad, back in the days when poles such as these were of little or no value for lumber. Despite the resounding title, the line served only as a logging railroad for the Peninsula Lumber Company, of Portland, in the area around Columbia City, Oregon.

H. G. Nelson photo from Labbe and Goe Collection

Top: Shay No. 2 of the Peninsula Lumber Company, at Columbia City, crosses a gulley on a bridge of cribbed logs. This was the Columbia and Nehalem Valley Railroad, about 1900.

R. S. Lindsay

Middle: This is a bridge! It isn't an engineering masterpiece, and it used up a lot of nice redwood logs, but it got the trains across. No doubt, at the time, it was the quickest and most economical way to get the job done. Scene is on the line of the Santa Cruz Lumber Company, near Boulder, California in some pretty rough country.

Bert Ward

Bottom: High timber bridge somewhere along the Columbia about 1907.

Opposite: Most popular roadbuilding machine with the early loggers was the pile driver. Earth-moving equipment was slow and impractical, and the loggers could build much faster and cheaper on low trestlework. This crew is building road for the Big Creek Logging Company near Knappa, Oregon.

Weister photo from Willard Evenson

Above: Benson is building track above Clatskanie with a light pile driver mounted on two disconnected trucks.

C. Kinsey photo from Rudy Larson

Left: There is more than one way to build a trestle, and if you haven't a pile driver handy, you can build it on the ground and hoist it into position with a donkey. Scene is the Hammond Lumber Company at Oak Point, Washington.

E. W. Anderson

Above: Pile driver building trestle for Sorenson Logging Company at Svensen, Oregon on the lower Columbia, about 1910.

J. G. Kilner

Right: The J. B. Miller Logging Company builds a bridge in the hills back of Cathlamet. A skyline is set up to carry the heavy timbers out to the construction site.

Hi Davis

Above: Pile driver crew building new trestle for the Big Creek Logging Company, Knappa, Oregon.

Below: Completed trestle with brand new grade being built into the green timber beyond Camp 9. Excursion picture on page opposite was taken later on this same spot.

Weister Co. from Roy McCourry

Right: Big Creek logs move up an incline near Camp 6. Tied on to the rear drawhead is a jillpoke to guard against a runaway if the line should break. The steel tipped pole is designed to dig into the ties if the weight of the load is thrown against it.

Below: Big Creek loggers and their families enjoying a picnic in the woods. The two locomotives have brought them up from the camps to the green timber just beyone Camp 9. The engines are positioned at each end of the train as a safety factor on the steep grades. This way there is no possibility of a car breaking away with its cargo of women and children.

Above: C. C. Masten train on a 10 per cent grade near Svensen about 1905.

Miller-Freeman Publications

Left: Trestle on Bell's operation on Deep River in Washington. The three pile bents must have been a bit shaky judging by the added braces here and there.

C. Swenson

Right: C. C. Masten Camp on Cox Creek, near St. Helens. Masten moved from Svensen to Cox Creek in 1907, and in 1910 the operation was sold to the Milton Creek Logging Company.

Elber Brown

Below High trestle on the line of the Milton Creek Logging Company out of St. Helens, Oregon. This operation was originally put in by C. C. Masten when he moved up from Svensen about 1907.

Elber Brown

Above: The Alger Logging Company logged in the hills just north of Skamokawa, Washington, on the lower Columbia River.

Doug Richter

Right: Camp and railroad of The Whitney Company cling precariously to the mountain side. Most of Tillamook County is rough country, and here along the Kilches River is no exception. The Whitney Company transferred their interests from Blind Slough on the Columbia River to Garibaldi on the Oregon coast in 1919.

G. B. Abdill

Below: Camp No. 2 of the Eufaula Company (Eastern & Western Lumber Company) near the head of Germany Creek, just west of Longview, Washington, about 1918.

W. B. Fowler

Above: The camp of the Portland Lumber Company nears Grays River, Washington, balances atop a sharp ridge. This was the former Saldern operation which was taken over in 1909.

Right: Moving day. Houses from the bachelor camp are slipped aboard cars for the move. These are from the Long-Bell camp on the old Oregon-American operation out of Vernonia, Oregon.

Gregory Kamholz

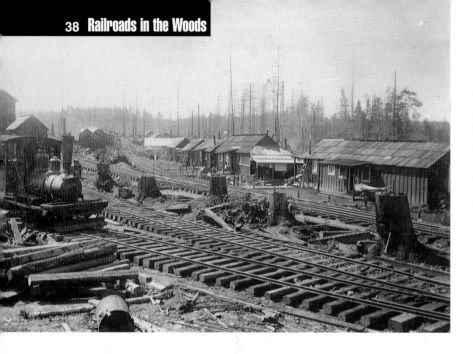

Top: Camp of the Portland Lumber Company, after they had bought out Yeon and Pelton late in 1905. By this time, the camp had moved to a point about midway between Rainier and Clatskanie, on the Beaver Creek watershed.

Babe Britton

Middle: Up and over. Milton Creek trains avoided a grade crossing with the Astoria and Columbia River, now the SP&S, with this overpass. Water tank in the distance marks the site of the St. Helens station.

Eber Brown

Bottom: Special timbers for the Panama Canal being brought out of the woods by Yeon and Pelton's little 4-spot.

J. F. Ford photo from Jim Brady

Above: Smith Powers Logging Company Shay No. 1 at a dump on the South Fork of Coos River in Coos County, Oregon. That fellow kneeling on the brow log would turn a safety engineer's hair gray.
John and George Powers

Below left: Milton Creek dump near St. Helens, Oregon. The apron was designed to protect the piling of the dump and to shoot the logs out into deeper water.
Eber Brown

Below right: The Yeon and Pelton No. 3 in Portland Lumber Company livery. When the No. 2 and the No. 3 were no longer serviceable, they were hauled down to the river and loaded aboard a ship for Japan.
Cecil Davis, Sr.

Above: Silverton Lumber Company's old woodburner pauses, but not for the photographer. Looks like the fourth load is down on the ties—a not unusual occurrence. Scene is in the Abiqua Valley northeast of Silverton, Oregon, where the line was laid out in 1907.

Drake photo from the Oregon Historical Society

Early Rails

Rails have always been one of the more expensive requisites of railroading. But when loggers could not afford steel rails they did without them. They made railroads of peeled poles instead, on which rode vehicles with large concave wheels to fit them. If they couldn't raise the price of a locomotive they used horses to pull the cars. More often they were able to gather together enough odds and ends, including a steam boiler, to assemble some sort of makeshift locomotive. If they could scrape together the price of an engine there were manufacturers ready and waiting to build one to fit the requirements of the road.

A slight improvement over the pole road was afforded by the wooden tram road. This was made by using sawn timbers for the rails, and it provided a smoother, more versatile, road in which it was possible to incorporate switches and sidings. An indication of the feasibility of this type of road may be gained from the following testimonial from C. C. "Charlie" Masten to the Climax Locomotive Company. Mr. Masten had purchased Climax No. 183 for his tram road at Svensen, Oregon. On March 1, 1899 he wrote:

> *"Having run my 15-ton locomotive recently purchased from you, for a period of thirty days, I am pleased to say it is doing more and better work than I ever expected a locomotive capable of doing on such a road as I have. My road is two and a quarter miles long, built of 8 × 8 sawed timber, seven foot gauge, with forty degree curves in places. I am hauling from 10,000 to 15,000 feet per load, making four trips per day, and can make six trips per day when we have the logs ready, and my doing all this work on the fast speed I have no hesitancy in recommending the 'Climax Locomotive' to anyone wanting a logging engine."*

Many of the early railroads were chartered as common carriers. No doubt this was often brought about by the prevailing railroad fever. Not a few of them probably had visions, as they laid their first rails, of burgeoning railroad empires. Perhaps, also, they found it easier to finance their dreams.

On the other hand, there were those who found it expedient for other reasons. There was Mr. Hobart, for instance, who spent much of the year 1890 laboriously constructing a six-foot gauge pole road between Falls City and Dallas, Oregon, that he might bring the raw materials from the woods to the Dallas mills. With his goal almost within reach he was frustrated by the denial of a short, but vital, stretch of right of way. In desperation he chartered his line as the Dallas and Ellendale Railway, and thus gained authority to condemn the land he needed.

At least one company was incorporated to provide a mainline railroad, but found the logging business so much more attractive it lost sight of its original goal. The Vancouver, Klickitat and Yakima was planned to serve the towns of Vancouver and Yakima by way of Klickitat Pass. It was envisioned as a transcontinental connection serving the lower Columbia River area, and its promoters had plans for developing various likely ore deposits along the way. The first few miles out of Vancouver were put in service early in 1889, and immediately the company turned to logging to support the further development of the road. But so engrossed did they become in this side line, the next few years saw the construction of but a mile or two of track a year. By the opening of the year 1891, Mr. P. C. McFarlane, the line's president, was moved to boast that the road was earning more per mile than any other in the state of Washington. Over the years this line has passed through several changes of ownership and was for many years a branch of the Northern Pacific. Early in 1960 the International Paper Company bought it from the Northern Pacific. The large Long-Bell mill at Longview is being transferred to Chelatchie Prairie above Yacolt, and the railroad subsidiary of the company, the Longview, Portland and Northern, will operate the line to serve the new mill. Thus, though the line never got much beyond the town of Yacolt, some forty miles out of Vancouver, it is still supported by forest products and still going strong.

Below: Logging railroad built in 1906 to serve the mill of the C. C. Wilson Lumber Company of Hudson, just west of Rainier, Oregon. Everything but the big wheels seems to have been put together on the spot. The rails are small poles, and the car is fastened to the engine with a chain. And when one boiler won't provide enough steam, the logical answer is two boilers.

Tom Timony

Right: A good example of the ingenuity shown by the early loggers. On the right is a makeshift locomotive built to operate on a railroad made of wooden poles. On the left is a donkey engine also designed to run on the pole road, anticipating by many years the commercial, rail-mounted skidders.

Mr. Richardson

Below: Early Climax locomotive designed to run on logs in lieu of rails. This pole road was operated by the Olympia Lumber Company in the Puget Sound country.

Robert Chaimberlain

Above: A wooden tram road near Marshland, Oregon, in 1902. Each truck of the car had four wheels, and a system of brakes was actuated by a block and tackle arrangement. With this setup the four horses could handle a fairly sizable load of logs. The horses were soon replaced by a small Shay on steel rails.

Mark Elliot

Right: The wooden tram road was a cut above the pole road. It could be built much like a railroad of steel and it could utilize similar equipment. This picture of the J. W. Winthrow Lumber Company of Tenino, Washington, shows how a switch was designed for wooden rails. Apparently the logs were transferred from the tram road to the regular railroad at this point, a rather unusual procedure.

Oregon Historical Society

Above: A type "A" Climax engine working in big fir along the lower Columbia River. This was C. C. Masten's operation near Svensen, Oregon. The engine was originally designed to run on a seven-foot gauge tram road made up of 8 × 8 sawn timbers. She was No. 183, and she was turned out for Masten in December 1898. Climax engines of this type were equipped with a gearbox, or selective transmission, which allowed the engineer a choice of gear ratios.
J. F. Ford photo from Miller-Freeman Publications

Below left: A little engine with a big history. She was No. 1236, built by the H. K. Porter Co. in 1891 as a 2-4-2 for Honeyman Hart & Co. of Medford, Oregon. She ran in passenger service between Medford and Jacksonville, Oregon, until 1895 when she was sold for service on the Albany, Oregon, street railway system. Here her pony truck was removed and she became an 0-4-2. She was ultimately used by the J. H. Chambers Lumber Company at Cottage Grove and was last used in 1946 by the Lorane Valley Lumber Company, successor to Chambers. She is now the property of a railfan and is preserved in Pasadena, California. In the photo, she is Lorane Valley Lumber Company No. 1, at Cottage Grove.
B. H. Ward

Below right: Allen's Mill railroad, near Little Rock, Washington, about 1902. If a logger couldn't afford to buy a locomotive he could often gather enough of the fundamentals to create one of his own. In this case the boiler came from China, while the engines and drive probably came from a discarded donkey. It did the job well—so well in fact that it was later sent up to work in Alaska.
C. W. Mendenhall

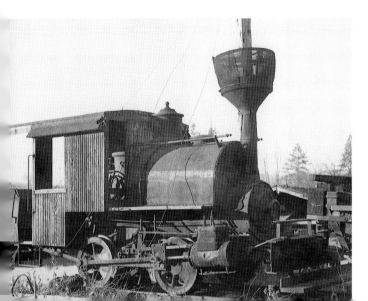

Above: Early passenger train of the Portland, Vancouver and Yakima being brought in by barge. The PV&Y was the successor to the original Vancouver, Klickitat and Yakima. Later it became the Yacolt branch of the Northern Pacific and in 1960 was taken over by the Longview, Portland and Northern, the railroad subsidiary of International Paper Company. Always supported by logs and lumber, in the days of the PV&Y the line still had hopes of becoming an important transcontinental link.

Oregon Historical Society

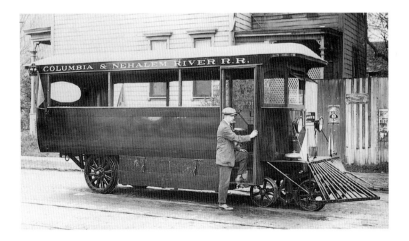

Left: Special motor car built for passenger service on the Columbia & Nehalem Valley Railroad, the "Kerry Line." She is shown on a city street in Portland, where she was built.

Angelus photo from D. L. Stearns

Above: Passenger service on the Portland and Southwestern? Well, not exactly. A real estate promoter was subdividing logged over land near Chapman, Oregon, and he arranged for the Chapman Timber Company line to handle picnic cars that came down from Portland on Sundays over the SP&S. He didn't sell many lots, but it was all free and lots of fun.

SP&S "Dope Bucket"

Right: Carlton and Coast No. 2 and an ancient coach pictured in Carlton, Oregon, in 1921. This old lokey was built by McKay and Aldus in 1868 and served the Central Pacific and Southern Pacific until it came to the Carlton and Coast in 1911.

George B. Abdill

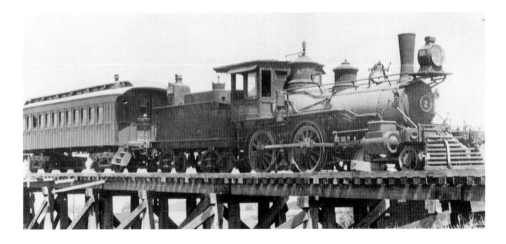

Above: An old Oregon and California Railroad Mogul was photographed at Onalaska, Washington in the early 1920's as she arrived for service on the line of Superior Log and Spar company. She was built by Baldwin about 1883.
Ben Griffiths photo from G. B. Abdill

Below: A primitive logging engine at work near Myrtle Point, Oregon, July 29, 1907. The early history of railroad logging in the Coos Bay area has never been wholly explored, but it seems certain that the first logging railroads in the Northwest were located in this area.
Oregon Historical Society

Above: This was the Grays Bay Logging Company, an early Brix brothers operation along Grays River, Washington. The locomotive was a Dunkirk, the only one known to have reached the west coast. George Vaughn was the engineer.
Cy Vaughn

Below: A Washington Northern Heisler switches the Blazier Logging Company dump deep in the gorge of the Columbia River. Famed Multnomah Falls is in the background.
Mr. Duggan

Above: Unusual rail mounted logging unit at work in the mountains southwest of Dunsmuir, California, for the Lamoine Lumber & Trading Company.
University of Oregon-Oregon Collections

Below: No 1. on the Washington Northern RR., of Blazier Logging Company heads a train of logs across a cribbed bridge in the Cascades just north of the Columbia.
Fred Froeschle photo from George Abdill

Top: Johnny Hepburn and his Shay pause for a picture on the Palmer Libby operation in the hills west of Westport, Oregon where he contracted the hauling with his own engine. Note the photographer's hamper in the foreground.

Coe photo from Mrs. McPherson

Middle: Heisler No. 3 of the Peninsula Lumber Company pauses on an impressive log bridge near Columbia City, Oregon. They must have found the headlight useful, because they have mounted it high in the air where it can clear a loaded car.

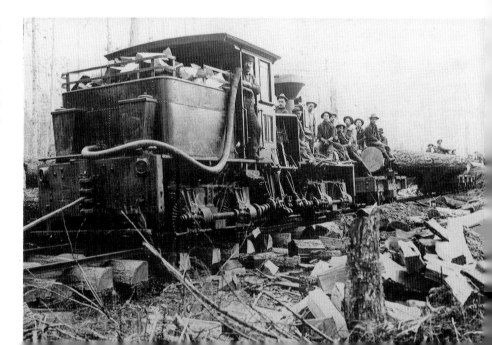

Bottom: Two cylinder Shay at Oak Point, Washington. George Badger was the engineer. Note the light rail and split ties. H. B. & A., incidentally, stood for Holland, Briggs and Avery, a title that was seldom heard. The company was formed in 1908 to deal in timberlands and turned to active logging here in 1910.

J. M. McClelland, Jr.

Above: Rough trackage typical of most of the small railroad shows that blanketed the Northwest. This was Bell's Camp on Deep River in Washington.

H. Swenson

Early Equipment

The tracks used by the average logging railroad were extremely light and flimsy. The lines were temporary, at best, and they were laid down with little regard to ballast and roadbed. Before the advent of modern earth moving equipment the logging engineer found it more economical and convenient to avoid excavating wherever possible. Logs, poles and lumber were cheap and plentiful, and roads were often built on shallow cribbing or trestlework. In search of an easy grade, many times they would build right up the bed of a creek on poles or logs. And when, after a few weeks of intense activity, the spur had been logged, the rail was pulled up and relaid in the next location. Yet over this rickety trackwork the loggers moved their cumbersome logging machines and their loaded cars of logs—loads that would have given a mainline railroader nightmares.

In the beginning the equipment was small and light. It had to be transported into out of the way places where no roads existed. Their little engines were floated up shallow rivers aboard barges; they were dismantled and piled into wagons to be carted over primitive trails, and sometimes they were loaded onto sleds and dragged back into the hills, making their own roads as they went.

Little four and six wheel tank engines were inexpensive to obtain and easily transported. Most of them were built by Baldwin or Porter, although anyone who built a small engine had a market and many local builders tried their hand at it. They burned wood, which was all around them, and they were devoid of such devices as brakes or lights. Simple as these engines were it was not surprising, therefore, that many hardpressed loggers were tempted to build their own.

The first steam donkeys made their appearance in 1885 when Dolbeer brought out his famous spool donkey. They were crude and inefficient, but they pointed the way to the great development of steam in the woods. And once this potential had been indicated developments were swift and dramatic. Early machines quickly became obsolete and were discarded in favor of newer improvements. Much of this early equipment was rebuilt into better logging machines. It also provided the ingredients for most of the homemade locomotives.

Another valuable source of motive power was provided by the street railway lines sprouting up in all the "progressive" towns and cities of the West. Horsecar lines were adequate to serve the business areas, but towns were spreading rapidly, and by the late 1880's a network of surburban lines was springing up served by steam motors. But almost before steam had become established here it was replaced by the new electric cars of the '90's. Much of this displaced steam equipment found its way to the woods.

The steam motors were essentially small tank engines disguised by the addition of a coach body that hid all but the driving sheels and the big stack. Designed for street service where the track was light and the curves sharp, they proved to be ideal for the logger's use. They were carried away and put to work in the woods without alteration. Seldom, even, was the awkward coach-like superstructure removed until the ravages of time and careless handling caused it to disintegrate.

The regular railroad flatcars with which many operators began hauling logs were soon abandoned in favor of the disconnected trucks. As the rails climbed further back into the mountains it became difficult to haul the heavy cars back up to the woods. The use of flatcars also required that the logs be cut to shorter lengths. This added greatly to the cost of logging and reduced the value of the logs, which often commanded premium prices for size and length.

The disconnected trucks could be adjusted to any length of log, limited only by the grade and curves to be negotiated. They were cheap to build and easy to transport. Usually the logger built them on the job and thus had only to bring the steel components with him. By reducing the load on the return trip they made it possible for the trains to work on steeper grades.

Early in the 1890's the Bridal Veil Lumbering Company made use of a narrow gauge railroad to close the gap between the bull teams and the mill. The country here at the western end of the Columbia River Gorge is steep and rugged. The mill at Palmer was connected with the finishing plant far below on the Union Pacific by a flume. The company acquired a little three foot gauge Baldwin tank engine and some flatcars and managed to get them into operation above the mill. "Peggy," as the little engine was called, was soon hard at work serving several sides on grades that reached seven per cent in places. A few hair-raising experiences with the loaded cars, however, inspired the company to look for safer methods of transport. They tried planking between the rails and hauling down the logs dogged together as for the bull teams. This experiment was so successful that cars were discarded on the steeper lines and the method was used for many years. It was later used by many other loggers in the Northwest. And while it seems a logical progression from the bull teams, the men at Bridal Veil took pride in having originated it.

Below: Before the coming of the bulldozer, grades were built with pick and shovel. Scene shows construction work on the line of the Silver Falls Timber Company east of Silverton, Oregon, where the company began building their railroad in 1912.

Drake Photo from Oregon Historical Society

Above: The average logging railroad was made up of secondhand rail used over and over again until it became too decrepit for any kind of service. Short pieces filling in at the joint were known as "Dutchmen." These pictures were taken along the line of the Deep River Logging Company in 1955.

S. B. Lawrence

Above right: Silver Falls Timber Company operation being excavated by laborers with pick and shovel east of Silverton, Oregon.

Drake photo from the Oregon Historical Society

Below right: Track gang at work on narrow gauge line of Yeon and Pelton.

J. F. Ford photo from Jim Brady

Left: Gypsy engine of the Indian Creek Lumber Company, of Moody, California. Originally she was the property of the South Humboldt Lumber Company. She had been stored for 35 years before being rolled outside for this photo. Note the tree growing between the rails.

B. H. Ward

Below: Little Porter engine used by Saldern at Grays River. He had earlier used it to log Fall Creek just below Clatskanie, Oregon. Billy Winters, the engineer, was taken to task for not keeping the bolts tight on the locomotive, but he insisted that it wouldn't stay on the poor track if it was tight. Instead, he carried a sack of nuts and bolts with which to replace those that fell off.

H. Swenson

Top: Climax No. 2, of the May Creek Logging Company, on a foggy morning. This operation was near the foot of Lake Washington, not far from Renton, Washington.

C. Wirkkala

Middle: Madera Sugar Pine Company at Madera, California. Besty, No. 1. was a 36-inch gauge geared engine of seven tons. She must have been a rough riding old girl, and the engineer must often have felt like a sea captain riding a poop deck.

B. H. Ward

Bottom: Mount Shasta Pine and Manufacturing Co., near Mount Shasta, California. The use of chains on the logs was largely confined to the pine country, seldom being found west of the Cascades. Unusual, too, is the arrangement of the brakewheels on the trucks. These sets of trucks are coupled together under the loads and are used as though they were regular flats. The brakewheels are located for the convenience of the brakeman, only two of the four trucks being equipped with them.

Bert Ward

Above: Headed into the hills far from civilization and railroads. Mounted on a sled, this Heisler is being transported overland by the donkey, and all they need for right of way is plenty of clearance between the stumps. This was the operation of the E. C. Shevlin Timber Company east of Kalama, Washington where operations were begun in 1909.

Miller-Freeman Publications

Left: Another way to move a locomotive without a railroad. The Santa Cruz Lumber Company makes use of a skyline to get this little Shay down into the floor of the valley where it has its railroad. Picture was taken near Boulder, California in 1930. The Shay arrived by truck, but the road was steep and treacherous and the skyline was the safe way of getting the job done.

Bert Ward

Right: Around the turn of the century Louis Saldern was logging the north slope of K-M Mountain, between Grays River and Skamokowa, in Washington. His logs were dumped into Grays River and rafted the tortuous miles down to the Columbia. And when, in 1900, he bought a brand new Climax to go with his little Porter tank engine, it had to be barged back up the same Grays River. Steam is up, and as soon as the track is spiked down the 2-spot will be on her way.

J. M. McClelland, Jr.

Below: View of the Ostrander Railway and Timber Company's dump along the Cowlitz River. The picture was taken from the overpass on the Northern Pacific mainline between Portland and Seattle. Notice the ramp at the right by which rolling stock was transferred to and from barges.

J. M. McClelland, Jr.

Above: A Willamette Shay-type engine loaded aboard a barge for delivery down the river. The Eufaula Company was the name Eastern and Western had conferred upon the old Mosquito and Coal Creek Railroad of B. F. Brock.

Left: Shay No. 9 of the Portland Lumber Company arrives at Grays River, Washington, about 1914. Grays River isn't much of a stream, but it is affected by the tidal action to a point near the community of Grays River and that was all the loggers needed. Working with the tides, large quantities of men and supplies came to Grays River on the little boats from Astoria—and many millions of feet of logs departed.

Right: This little Climax of the Snow Creek Logging Company is being moved into the hills back of Sequim, Washington, under its own power circa 1914. The great flexibility of the Climax design allowed it to negotiate the roughest trackwork with comparative ease.

Thomas T. Taber III

Below: A Vancouver Lumber Company Climax at work at Port Neville Camp in British Columbia. The cedar logs are being skidded between the rails, although in this post World War I period the practice was almost obsolete.

Miller-Freeman Publications

Top and Middle: Bringing out some big logs for the Cathlamet Logging Company along the lower Columbia River just west of Cathlamet, Washington. The lokey came from the City & West Portland Park Motor Company line between Portland and Multnomah. She was Baldwin No 11528, built in January 1891 as their No. 2. She had 35-inch drivers and 11 × 16-inch cylinders, and she was well suited for work on a small logging railroad.

Top: V. V. Vinson photo from the Labbe and Goe collection.
Middle: G. B. Abdill.

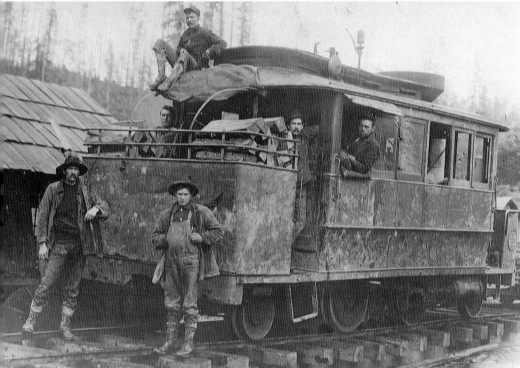

Bottom: Steam dummy at work near Boring, Oregon about 1900.

Mrs. Cora Yandel

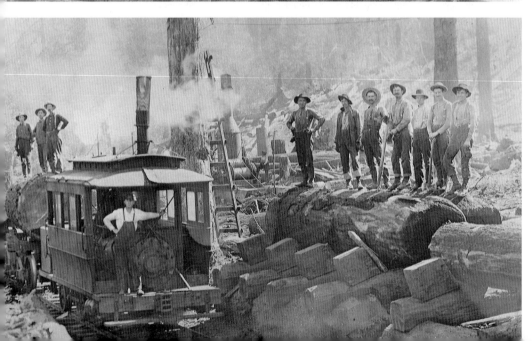

Above: The little loco which began life as a steam dummy on the Independence & Monmouth Railway at Independence, Oregon, trundled back and forth from the dump with a single car.

Hi Davis

Below: Little steam dummy known as the "Katy" at the pond of Mill A of the Oregon Lumber Company near Cook, Washington, about 1903. She is believed to have come from Ogden, Utah, and she worked on grades so steep that it is said that on the last pitch to the rollway she had to have the help of two men pushing to make it over the top.

G. B. Abdill Collection

Left: An old steam dummy of the Cathlamet Logging Company at work in the woods along the Lower Columbia. A graphic illustration of the little dummy's ability to snake around sharp curves on light rail. The track has been laid right up the bed of the creek to eliminate as much excavating as possible.

Mrs. Burns

Above: Yeon and Pelton's line-up of rod engines. They all came from Portland Street Railways where they were bought new by the Willamette Bridge Railway Company as dummies. Front to rear are No. 3, Baldwin No. 9973, built in April 1889; No. 2, Baldwin No. 9847, built in February 1889; and No. 4, Baldwin No. 10683, built in March 1890. Building in the rear is where the loads were prepared for the trip down the incline.

Left: Engineer Harry Coleman stops at the water plug with the 2-spot.

4 pictures: J. F. Ford photos from Jim Brady

Above: Harry Coleman and the Yeon and Pelton 2-spot moving a donkey. In the foreground next to the stump is John Yeon.

Right: Yeon and Pelton track gang about 1907.

Top: A good example of why the loggers preferred to use disconnected trucks. The flats used here are too short for hauling long logs. They have been adapted for longer loads by the addition of log bunks, but the equipment is still too heavy and awkward for the job. This scene is on the line of the Columbia Timber Company, near Goble, Oregon.

Left: Wooden disconnected trucks, such as these, were built right on the job. Only the hardware had to be carried into the woods.

Jim Brady

Left: A variety of wooden disconnects. Note that they vary considerably and must remain in matched sets. Note also that the one engaging the man's attention is off the rail—an occurrence that happened all too frequently.

Jim Brady

Bottom: Seaside Spruce Lumber Company at Seaside, Oregon. These crude trucks have neither springs nor brakes. The rod engine came from the Astoria and Columbia River Railroad.

C. Ahlers photo from J. G. Kilner

Left: The donkey puncher bears down on the friction lever as he swings a log from the cold deck to the car. Scene is near Deep River, Washington, on the Deep River Logging Company's operation.

J. F. Ford photo from Jens Lerbach and Fred Hendrickson

Below: A two-drum Willamette donkey drags the logs to the roll-way where they are rolled aboard the flat cars for the trip to the mill. Scene is thought to be Bridal Veil.

Above: Bridal Veil Lumbering Company log train, in the hills east of Portland, back in the days when they still rolled the logs on by hand. No. 1 was one of two small Baldwin tank engines used on the narrow gauge line. But in spite of the No. 1, she was not the first engine at Bridal Veil. She was preceded by "Peggy," who handled the operation all alone for several years.

University of Oregon Collection

Left: "Peggy" as she looked after being caught in a forest fire in 1902. Engineer Jesse Everhart has to get by without his cab, and Fireman Faust has a flatcar to take the place of the little single truck tender—but in spite of it all Peggy is still on the job.

J. H. McMilan

Right: "Peggy," in the early 1890's. The log cars were soon found to be too risky on the steep grades, and the logs were dogged together and skidded between the rails.

J. H. McMilan

Below: Bridal Veil tank engine with a mixed train. Logs behind the engine are loaded on flatcars, while those ahead of the engine are being skidded between the rails.

Oregon Historical Society

Above: Mill of the Bridal Veil Lumbering Company at Palmer about 1895. "Peggy" has just brought a turn of logs down to the dump. The logs have been brought out of the woods by bulls and skidded down to the mill between the rails. Note the engine house in the right background.

D. L. Stearns

Left: "Peggy" gets ready to take another turn of logs from the holding pond down to the mill at Palmer along about 1895. "Peggy" served several sides, and the trestle in the distance goes to one of them, while directly under it can be seen the chute by which logs arrive in the pond from one of the others. Notice the planks between the rails of the track on which the logs slide.

Collection of Dave Stearns and John Labbe

Right: Interior view of the shops of the Cathlamet Timber Company. This was typical of the many small shops that kept the donkeys and the locomotives in repair. It was shared by the blacksmith who kept the logger's gear serviceable, as can be seen in the foreground.

H. S. Turley

Below: Simpson Logging Company's "Tollie." This little Heisler, the first to arrive on the west coast, was used for dragging the logs from the yarder to the landing, where they were rolled aboard cars for the final trip. Tollie dragged the logs along the ties. The engine was named for Sol Simpson's wife and was fired by Bill Grisdale, nephew of Sol Simpson, when he first arrived in 1898. The name "Tollie" is still preserved, having been given to the large, three-truck Shay placed on display in Shelton, Washington, by the Company.

Kirk & Collier photo from the Oregon Historical Society

Above: Bell's No. 2 pauses in the rain forest along Deep River in Washington on the lower Columbia. Cecil Hurd was the engineer.

Arthur M. Prentiss photo from Labbe and Goe collection

Geared Engines

Hard on the heels of the little rod engines came the geared engines. These were specifically designed to meet the problems of the logger. They were designed to give maximum tractive effort with minimum weight. Speed was sacrificed to power, and flexibility was their hallmark.

Three manufacturers dominated the field of the geared engines. Of these three the Shay was undoubtedly the most popular locomotive used by Western loggers. Ephraim Shay, who was responsible for the design, was himself a Michigan logger. He knew the logger's problems and designed an engine to handle them. The Lima Locomotive Works never had occasion to regret the day that Ephraim Shay came to them with his plans. Over the years they built hundreds of geared engines, and the Lima Shay became an institution around the world.

The Shay made use of a vertical engine of three cylinders mounted just ahead of the cab on the right-hand side. Connected to the crankshaft was a lineshaft that carried the power to all the axles. Provided with slip joints and universals, the lineshaft was flexible enough to allow the trucks full freedom of movement under the engine frame. Bevel gears on the shaft and on the face of the right-hand wheel transmitted the power. The moving parts were easily accessible for servicing and shims in the axle journals allowed for easy adjustment of the driving gears.

The most notable characteristic of the Shay was its boiler. In order to compensate for the weight and position of the engines the boiler was set over to the left of the center line, giving it an odd, lop-sided appearance. Another distinctive feature was the engine itself. The left-hand cylinder carried its steam chest on the left side while the other two faced right, and the rapid rhythm of this three cylinder exhaust became part and parcel of the logging scene. No one who has ever known it could forget it. A Shay thrashing its slow course up a heavy grade was lost in an aura of sound and smoke and steam.

The Shay was an easy riding engine and it was rugged and durable. It might strew the right of way with discarded parts, and its gears might be nearly devoid of teeth, but little short of complete derailment could thwart its progress.

No engine used in the woods was available in such profuse variety. Varying in size from tiny narrow gauge teakettles to huge mainline machines, they were designed for hundreds of specific jobs. Some had two trucks, some had three—or even four. For variety, some of the smaller engines had but two cylinders. So flexible was this design that of the 2,761 engines turned out between 1880 and 1945 it is difficult to find two alike.

In the late 1920's Lima brought out the Pacific Coast model. This was a 90-ton three-truck engine designed especially for West Coast loggers. It incorporated such refinements as a super heater and piston valves. The purpose was to provide an engine incorporating the savings inherent in a standardized model of advanced design. So successful was the Pacific Coast that several are still in daily service, and it is not inconceivable that there might be a market for them today if they were available.

Second of the geared engines in popularity was the Climax. The Climax came to the woods of the Pacific Northwest soon after the loggers had taken to rails. The first Climax used in the West was bought by Mr. Hobart for his Dallas and Ellendale Railway. It was a Class A built in June of 1891. It was delivered and put to work the following month on Mr. Hobart's six foot gauge pole road.

This early Class A Climax made use of a vertical two cylinder marine-type engine. However, unlike the Shay, this was mounted in the centerline of the frame behind the backhead. The lineshaft ran through the center of the engine, driving each of the axles through a pair of bevel gears. These engines also incorporated a selective transmission which gave the engineer a choice of gear ratios. Some of the very early Climax engines, Mr. Hobart's among them, used a vertical boiler very similar to those used on the donkey engines.

The later engines, which became familiar to loggers everywhere, had their cylinders mounted at an angle on either side of the smokebox. They drove a cross shaft just ahead of the cab which, in turn, was geared to the center driveshaft. The cylinders were not large, but with the reduced gearing employed they provided plenty of power and used a minimum of steam. Most engines built by the Climax company were of the two-truck design, although in later years they produced many of the large three-truck engines. Generally speaking they were lighter than the other engines while holding their own in pulling power. Of the three main designs, they were probably the slowest.

Many companies included a Climax in their rosters for special jobs but few companies bought them in quantity. The flying mainrods had a tendency to set up a vibration in the engine that crews disliked. It was claimed by their detractors that a Climax would disintegrate itself, the railroad and the engine crews with equal impartiality. With the passing of the years a Climax tended to develop a sag in the middle—but to their credit let it be added that they built up an impressive record for service and reliability.

The third of the great triumvirate was the Heisler locomotive. It was the last to make its appearance but it proved a popular and useful engine. As with the Climax, early engines were of the two-truck variety while later designs were more often of the larger three-truck type. Aside from the fact that Heisler offered a wide choice of weights and sizes, there was little to distinguish one engine from another. Heisler probably came closer to standardizing its product than any other locomotive manufacturer.

The Heisler made use of a center driveshaft, although it differed greatly from the Climax in all other respects. The driveshaft was geared to the outer axle in each truck and siderods mounted on the face of the wheels carried the power to the second axle. The two large cylinders were mounted in a 'V' just ahead of the cab and drove the crankshaft which was a part of the driveshaft.

The locomotive was designed to perform much like a rod engine while retaining the advantages of a geared engine. It was capable of fair speeds on good track and rode very well on poor track. The faster performance, which tended to reduce its effectiveness on heavy grades, was off-

Left: Shays came in all sizes, but it is doubtful if they came much smaller than this little kettle. She was No. 2590, a two-cylinder job turned out by Lima in 1912 as No. 1 of the Molino Timber Company, of Loma Prieta, California. Gauge of the line was thirty inches.

Doug Richter

set by an unusually large cylinder. There were times when this taxed the steaming capacity of the boiler, but generally speaking, the Heisler was an eminently successful engine.

One other geared engine made a brief but impressive appearance on the logging scene. Following World War I, when the Willamette Iron and Steel Works, of Portland, Oregon, found itself with a greatly enlarged plant and staff, they made a determined effort to keep production up to full capacity. Taking advantage of the fact that the Shay patents had become public property they began to produce a locomotive of their own, patterned closely after the Lima Shay.

The first Willamette engine was delivered to Coos Bay Lumber Company late in 1922. Between that time and the end of the year 1929, 33 engines were built and delivered to western companies. Two of these were two-truckers of about 50 tons. All of the others were of the three-truck design and weighed between 75 and 80 tons.

Right: The oldest Shay around. This little two cylinder engine with the "T"-shaped boiler was built for the Rumsey Lumber Company of Big Rapids, Michigan, in 1884. She was Lima No. 122. She saw service on the three-foot gauge line of the Michigan-California Lumber Company until 1949, when she was put on display near the company offices at Camino, California.

B. H. Ward

Right: This standard gauge Shay was working around Jacobson and Reed's sawmill in the hills back of Rainier, Oregon, as late as 1917. She was a two-cylinder job, and somewhere along the way she picked up some homemade sanders on her tank. No one worried too much about fire in those days, as neither the little woodburner nor the mill fire boasted a screen.

Tom Timony

Above: Lima Shay No. 559 was built for Benson of Oak Point, Washington, in 1898. Benson normally retained the builder's numbers for his engine numbers. Note the split ties and light rail.

Miller-Freeman Publications

Below: Resplendent in a new coat of paint, Lima No. 884, Benson Logging and Lumber Company's No. 884, shows off her new number under her new owners, although she is still working the same show at Midway Landing along the Washington side of the Columbia. Under the cab window she carries the name "Black Bessie." Not long after this picture was taken a runaway train of logs piled up around the 3-spot in camp. It didn't end her career, but it ruined the pretty paint job.

J. M. McClelland, Jr.

Top: Lima No. 671, one of Benson's early Shays at Oak Point. The No. 671 turned out to be quite a boomer, working for many years along the river for a number of different owners.

Arthur Clarkson

Middle: No. 1 of the Western Pine Company, at Klickitat, Washington. This little 2-cylinder machine was built by Lima in 1910.

Norman Elsner

Bottom: Lima Shay No. 779, built for Benson Logging and Lumber Company in 1903, is shown here at the dump at Clatskanie, Oregon. Simon Benson owned a great many Shays over the years, but this was his only three-trucker—and he didn't keep it around very long.

Elite Studio from Colvin's Tavern, Clatskanie

Above: Spaulding Miami Lumber Company No. 7 stands ready to pull the first train of logs out of Grande Ronde, Oregon. The date is November 25, 1921 and William Lentz is the engineer. But, though the line was new, the old woodburner was not. She was built way back in 1900 for the Phoenix Logging Company up on Hood Canal in Washington state.

University of Oregon collection

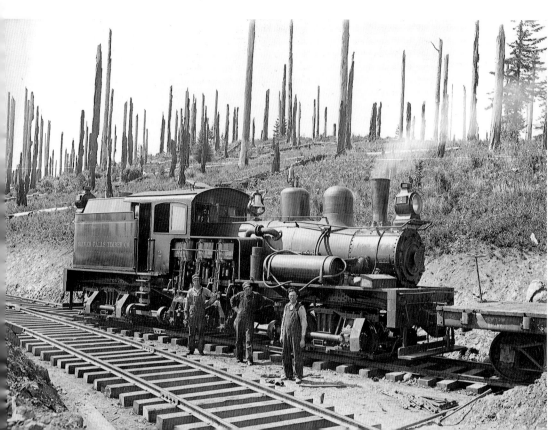

Left: Trim little 2-spot of the Silver Falls Timber Company.

Drake photo from Oregon Historical Society

Above: This big Shay was built in 1894 and sold to the Newaukum Valley R.R., Napavine, Washington. She is shown here as she passed through Portland on her way to Napavine. The Newaukum Valley ultimately extended to Onalaska.

Lamar Ferguson

Right: The same engine as she looked in 1932 after considerable updating. She now carries the name of the Carlisle Lumber Company on her tank, but she hasn't left Onalaska.

D. S. Richter

Left: Flora Logging Company No. 8 in the hills west of Carlton, Oregon. Fireman Gil Gary in the doorway. Brakeman Cecil Davis seated on the runningboard.

C. Kinsey photo from Cecil Davis

Below: The Spaulding Logging Company's 5-spot takes time out from a busy schedule to have her picture taken. She was built in 1907 for the Salem, Falls City and Western, but she spent most of her life around Spaulding operations. The little woodburner is spic and span, which would indicate that she gets plenty of attention from her proud crew.

University of Oregon collection

Top: Big Creek Logging Company No. 2 in the hills south of Knappa, Oregon. The only three-truck Shay this company ever owned. She was wrecked after a short period of service. *J. G. Kilner*

Right: "Pacific Coast" type Shay at work for J. Neils Lumber Company of Klickitat, Washington. This beautifully maintained engine is still in service. *Walt Grande*

Below: Rayonier No. 191 was a Pacific Coast type Shay, built by Lima in 1930. Shown here in the spotless condition typical of all equipment at Railroad Camp near Hoquiam, Washington, she was cut up soon after the picture was taken.

Above: Undoubtedly the largest Shay used in the western woods was this big four-trucker of the Red River Lumber Company. The 300 is pictured here at Westwood, California, in May of 1936. She was a tricky engine to handle, as she had a tendency to pull everything off the track on sharp curves, a practice commonly referred to as "daisy-chaining."

L. Harrison

Above: White River Lumber Company No. 4, a Lima "Pacific Coast" Shay, near Enumclaw, Washington, in 1948.
Albert Farrow

Below: Small Shay of the Sunset Logging Company at Timber, Oregon. She was picked up secondhand in Portland after being given an overhaul and a fresh coat of paint.
George B. Abdill

The Climax

The Class A Climax was one of the early answers to the loggers' problem. These engines were offered with concave wheels to operate on pole roads and specially designed wheels for use on wooden tram roads, as well as conventional wheels for steel rails. The first models made use of a wooden frame (above) but heavier demands brought forth the steel frame (below). The engines met with immediate acceptance, and variations of the Class A were produced for many years after the later-style engines (Class B and C) were in production.

A. C. Graves

Right: The power plant of the Class A was obviously copied from a double-simple marine tugboat engine. The counterbalanced crankshaft made for smooth high-speed running. A lever (not shown) slid the gears on the keyed shaft to obtain two ratios for variable power.

A. C. Graves

Below: Builder's photo of a Class A Climax. Cylinders were mounted vertically at the rear of the cab. Gear ratios could be changed by the engineer by means of a sliding gear. This particular engine represents the last type of Class A built, about the middle of 1927, for service in Australia.

Lamar Ferguson

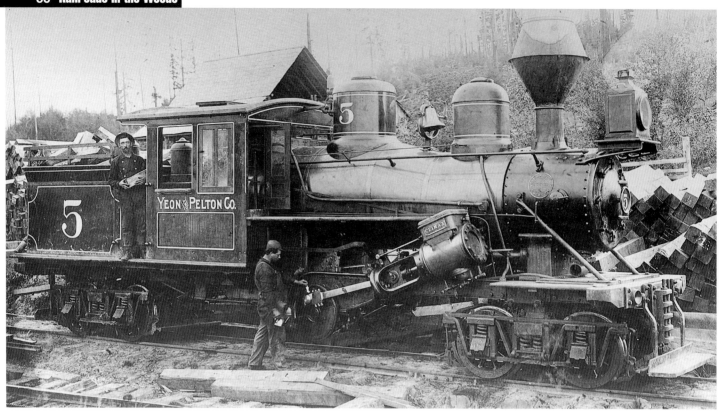

Above: This Climax was the first new engine purchased for the Yeon and Pelton operation, near Rainier, Oregon, and the first geared engine on the job. Previously, all of the lokeys came secondhand from the Portland street railways, which accounted for the gauge of 42 inches. No. 5 was Climax No. 457, built in 1904.
Willis Gulker

Below: The same engine under Portland Lumber Company ownership. She has been converted to an oilburner and renumbered—and without the spark arrester the short stack gives her an odd appearance. The chains on the drawbar are designed to keep it from dropping to the ground if the pin should inadvertently slip out.
Cecil Davis, Jr.

Left: Class A wood frame Climax No. 405 was sold to Bremner Logging Company of Astoria in June of 1903. Later the little 18-ton lokey was used by Crown-Willamette Paper Company on Young's River.

Harold M. Brown photo from Miller-Freeman Publications

Below: Small Climax used during construction at Silver Falls Timber Company, of Silverton, Oregon.

Drake photo from the Oregon Historical Society

Left: Vest pocket Climax—still in service when this picture was taken. She was number 407, built in 1903 for B.F. Brock's Mosquito and Coal Creek R.R. at Eufaula on the Columbia. After serving a number of owners over the years, she ended up here in Stanwood, Washington, as Hall and Hall No.1.

C. W. Mendenhall

Below: Crown-Willamette Paper Company No. 3. A 42-ton Climax built in 1915. Crown bought her in July of 1918 for $16,900. She was scrapped in 1949.

B. H. Ward

Above: Crown-Willamette Paper Company No. 4 in the woods of Wahkiakum, Washington. Originally operating out of Seaside, Oregon, as No. 5, she was transferred to the Washington side of the Columbia and renumbered No. 4. This is a late design, three-truck Climax, representing the ultimate from the Corry, Pennsylvania shops.
Miller-Freeman Publications

Below: This three-truck Climax was built for Bloedel-Donovan Lumber Mills at Bellingham, Washington. It is representative of the larger engines built by the Climax company
Lamar Ferguson

The Heisler

Below: Oscar Johnson relaxes in his cab as he keeps a sharp eye on the crew that is loading a log car out of the pond. His engine is a sixty-ton Heisler, No. 1198, built for Hammond Lumber Company of Mill City, Oregon, in March 1910. On this August day in 1955 she is nearing the end of her career, but she is still working in the same place for the Vancouver Plywood Company. This view of her gives an idea of the workings of a Heisler.

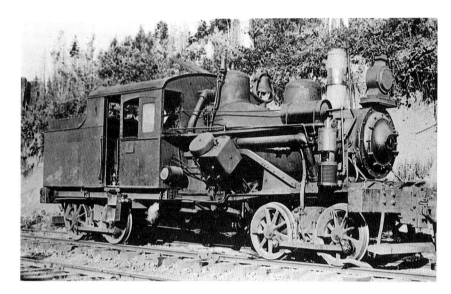

Right: Small two-truck Heisler No. 1148 of the Berst & Cox Logging Company near Timber, Oregon.

George B. Abdill

Below: Rare shot of a Heisler with a pilot. Peninsula Lumber Company's No. 3 was still brand new when this picture was taken near Columbia City, Oregon. The pilot didn't last long.

Robert Lindsey

Opposite above: Neat little Heisler of the Oregon Timber and Logging Company. This company logged an area just east of Nicholai Mountain and west of Westport, Oregon, and the logs were carried down to the dump at Clifton. Despite the size of the operation, the company never used more than two locomotives at any one time. The other engine was a Shay.

J. G. Kilner

Opposite below: A Heisler crests the top of an abrupt rise with a train of logs. She's No. 103 of the Mountain Timber Company of Kalama, Washington.

University of Oregon Collection

Below: The Vancouver Plywood Company No. 2 switching the reload at the pond in Mill City, Oregon, on an August day in 1955. This venerable Heisler has spent her lifetime on the trackage around Mill City, and she still puts in a day or two a week.

Above: Potlatch Forest No. 91, a three-truck Heisler, pictured here at Lewiston, Idaho in 1948. Note that the side rods have been removed for transit.
Lamar Ferguson

Below: Smith Powers No. 8, a three-truck Heisler, at work near Powers, Oregon. This engine once dropped through a bridge, killing four men. She went from Powers to Lorane Valley Lumber Company at Cottage Grove.
Dick Buike

Above: Heisler's answer to the Lima "Pacific Coast Shay." Heisler No. 1573, pictured here, was turned out in 1928 as the "New Class 90 West Coast Special." She went to Mud Bay Logging Company, a Weyerhaeuser subsidiary near Olympia, Washington.
Miller-Freeman Publications

Below: Big woodburning Heisler of the Wisconsin Logging and Timber Company. Part of her neat appearance is due to the running boards along the entire length of the boiler. Wisconsin bought out Benson's operation along Abernathy Creek on the north bank of the Columbia about 1906, and the 1-spot was put to work between the incline and the dump at Midway Landing. It was behind this engine that Vernon Goe got his first experience as a brakeman.
J. M. McClelland, Jr.

The Willamette

Below: The Willamette Iron and Steel Company shops did much service work on all types of logging engines. Here we see a Lima Shay fresh from the backshop, while just behind it a Willamette engine takes shape.

Above: Worm's eye view of the Coos Bay No. 10, the first Willamette engine, as she was being put through her paces short-ly after delivery.

Below: This was the second, and last, two-truck engine built by Willamette. She was No. 30, delivered on April Fool's Day in 1927. Fredrickson sold her to Cobbs and Mitchell, and she finished her career in the woods around Valsetz, Oregon.

Below: Scene in the shops of the Willamette Iron and Steel Company showing locomotives and a skidder under construction.

Left: View of the backhead of the first Willamette locomotive—Coos Bay Lumber Co. No. 10.

Below: Willamette engine No. 25, the first of the two-truckers built in Portland. This one went to the East Side Logging Company at Keasey, Oregon, and later to Sunset Logging Company at Timber, Oregon, as their No. 25. She was scrapped at Timber about 1950.

ANDERSON & MIDDLETON LUMBER COMPANY

MULTNOMAH LUMBER & BOX CO.

Top: Willamette locomotive No. 21 was turned out in April 1926. After serving Anderson Middleton, at Cottage Grove, she went to Westfir, Oregon, for the Edward Hines Lumber Company. Later Hines sold her to the Medford Corporation, where she became their No. 7. With the end of rail service in the woods, Medco reserved her for display in the city of Portland where she was never delivered and is now resting in Dunsmuir, California.

Middle: Willamette locomotive No 6 was built in May, 1923 for service on the old Spruce Division line out of Newport. She later went to Clark and Wilson, and then to Medford. The Medford Corporation turned her over to the scrappers in the spring of 1959, but she had been out of service for some time.

Bottom: Willamette locomotive No. 27 went to Sterling City, California. She was turned out in March of 1927. She later went to Clark and Wilson Lumber Company at Scappoose, Oregon, and then to Medford.

The Baldwin

The Baldwin Locomotive Works undoubtedly built more rod engines for use in the woods than any other manufacturer—everything from tiny tank engines to big articulateds. The proven efficiency of the geared engines for much of the work in the woods was a challenge to Baldwin designers. However, for one reason or another, Baldwin was never able to compete successfully for this business. Lima, Climax and Heisler were well established before Baldwin entered the picture, and design defects, coupled with adverse business conditions, combined to discourage Baldwin from becoming a serious competitor. The early engines, of which four were built, resembled the Climax in design. The fifth engine, pictured below, was built in 1915 and reflects the influence of the Shay. It has three cylinders lying horizontal beneath the boiler. They drive a shaft along the right-hand side of the frame, which, by means of bevel gears and jack shafts, transfers the power back across the trucks to drive the geared wheels on the left-hand side. A real monster, it marked the end of Baldwin's attempts in this field.

B. H. Ward

Above: This graceful two-trucker was a meter gauge turned out by Baldwin in 1914 for the Leopoldina Railway of Brazil. She was No. 41349—the fourth and last engine of this design built by Baldwin. Part of her trim appearance is due to the lack of a sand dome. Sanders appear to be incorporated in the trucks.

B. H. Ward

Below: The second Baldwin geared engine was sold to the Marysville and Northern, of Sedro Wooley, Washington. Patterned after the style of the Climax, it was one of two three-truckers built, but they were not a smashing success.

D. S. Richter

Above: Henry Colvin, in bowler hat and beard, mans the controls of the first Gripwheel. Pulling itself up and down the track along the cable visible next to the logs, this machine brought out many thousand feet. The trailer carried an emergency supply of wood, in case she didn't make it to one of the strategically located trackside woodpiles. A lot of hard work went into the sturdy trackwork.

Mrs. Kelty

The Gripwheel

Shortly after the advent of the steam donkey engine, George A. Fouts patented his famous Gripwheel. This was a device incorporated in a large wheel which gripped a wire rope as it turned. It was arranged in such a way that the gripping action took place only in one half of the cycle, the cable being released as the mechanism passed through the second half. With this machine, it was claimed, great savings in time could be effected, since there was no time lost in returning the rigging to the woods. It worked as an endless cable, allowing one log to follow another in quick succession, so long as the machine was capable of handling them.

Fouts also recommended the use of the Gripwheel as a locomotive, in which instance it would pull itself back and forth along a cable fixed between the rails. Attractive as this arrangement might seem it met with little acceptance by the loggers. The Colvins, of Marshland, Oregon, seem to have been the only ones to use it successfully.

It was about 1897 that Henry Colvin made his first trips with his Gripwheel. He had been logging along OK Creek with bulls, and the trip across the marshy ground to the nearest slough was giving the huge beasts a good deal of trouble. He reasoned that if he could lay rails across the swampy section, he could keep the bulls at work on the hill where they were best suited, and thereby increase the efficiency of his operation.

Rails were laid to a gauge of ten feet along the old skids of the bull road, and soon the Gripwheel was hard at work lugging the turns of logs to the water. At the dump the track was tilted to allow the logs to roll into the water, but if they failed to do so, Henry had merely to reverse his machine and shear them in as he returned.

The Gripwheel was a great success, although the Colvins, who had a mechanical turn of mind in common with most loggers, soon devised a number of improvements. The performance on the level going was so encouraging it was soon given a try on a grade. Here again it proved successful, and before long the Gripwheel was following the bulls up the steep canyon of OK Creek.

This first machine consisted of a small donkey boiler mounted on a platform and supported by four trucks. Each of these trucks consisted of two flanged wheels mounted on either end of an equalizing bar which was fastened rigidly to a corner of the mainframe of the machine. The two cylinders lay horizontally along the floor behind the vertical boiler.

Since there was no provision for brakes, other than that provided by the grip on the cable and the reversing action of the engine, large rocks were placed between the skids to hold back the logs on the grade. However, operation of the first machine was brought to an untimely end on the day when the slack was allowed to accumulate and the line ran out of the grip. No logs had yet been tied on to hold her on the hill and she ran away and was wrecked. The boiler and engines were later salvaged for use as a donkey, but the Gripwheel was not rebuilt.

Nevertheless, the first machine had proven itself to be both useful and practical, and the Colvins were anxious to build another machine incorporating all the improvements they had visualized out of their experience. A second machine was built by Willamette Iron and Steel Company, of Portland-larger and more powerful. A much larger boiler was used and the cylinders lay alongside the firebox.

The trucks were similar, but heavier, and the wheels were double flanged to compensate for the very poor track. Most important of all, a guide was devised to keep the line from ever again running out of the grip. Like the first machine, this one was fueled with wood from piles strategically located along the right of way. A platform extension at the rear carried an emergency supply.

And one further refinement was added-an emergency brake in the form of a steel tipped wooden beam that was hinged from the frame so that the steel tip dragged along the crossties.

On at least one occasion this emergency brake prevented a catastrophe. The line picked up a rock that cut it in two as it passed through a sheave. The Gripwheel started running free as the device bounced over the first few ties. When it finally caught and held, the sudden stop threw the operator clear over the woodpile at the rear—but it saved the machine.

This second Gripwheel was very powerful, averaging about 25,000 feet of logs to a run, and on at least one occasion coming in with 48,000 feet. The grade up OK Creek was 24 per cent, and the total distance worked was something over three miles.

A nephew of Henry Colvin was employed on the line to keep the skids greased and the hill clear of the bark scraped from the logs by the big rocks used for braking. He tells of one time when Henry attempted to bring down a train before the hill had been completely cleared. The drag of the piled up bark bogged down the engine, and in order to get some slack for a new start the Gripwheel had to force some of the logs back up the hill. Having jammed four or five of them together he "widened out" on the throttle in an attempt to get them moving again. But he pulled his train in two and soon found himself racing down the hill out of control. Fortunately no damage was done and he was able to proceed to the dump. However, when he returned for the second half of the train he was faced with another problem. The frame of the machine was used to hold the logs back on the grade, and the log now confronting him was too small to reach the frame. In order to keep it from running underneath and knocking out his ashpan he once more found himself racing down the hill at full speed.

When the Colvins sold out to the OK Logging Company the new owners had the machine considerably rebuilt under the supervision of the Willamette Iron and Steel Company. The gripwheel was removed and a drum substituted. Three wraps of the cable around the drum provided sufficient traction for the machine. The designer of this improvement was not able to sell it to the new owners until he had agreed to take no pay unless it proved entirely satisfactory. At this time, too, track brakes were added and the trucks were redesigned and reinforced.

In its final reincarnation the Gripwheel became known as the "Walking Dudley." The term was not new, having been applied to some similar machines designed and built by the Simpson Logging Company, of Shelton, Washington. The name was said to have come from an old logger who walked from camp to camp until he became known as "Walking Dudley."

Willamette built at least one other Dudley which was used at Pokegama, near Klamath Falls. This operation made use of a spectacular log chute into the Klamath River, and the Walking Dudley was used to nudge reluctant logs on their way down the chute.

Right: The Gripwheel at the dump. She has just pulled a turn of logs into the water with a cable dogged into the end of the last log. Note the cable by which she pulled herself along. Railroad in the background is the SP&S line to Astoria, then the Astoria and Columbia River Railroad.

Miller-Freeman Publications

Below: Second version of the Gripwheel, built after the original machine was wrecked. Clumsy as it appears, it did a good job. Working on grades as steep as 24 per cent, it averaged about 25,000 feet of logs to a turn.

Below: After the Colvins sold out to the OK Logging Company, the original Gripwheel was scarcely recognizable in this big machine. The original gripwheel is gone and many improvements and refinements have been added. Even the name has changed, and now it is called a "Walking Dudley."

Jesse Ebert photo from F. Hal Higgins

Above: Coast Range Lumber Company at Mabel, Oregon. The trestle was 176 feet high.
George Morrice

Below: Spars for the Kaiser's yacht. They were gotten out by the Mason County Logging Company for a spar company on Grays Harbor.
J. T. Buckley

Left: Shay No. 1 of the San Vincente Lumber Company scurries across a trestle near Swanton, California. And just in time, too. Shortly after this picture was taken the trestle collapsed from vibrations set up by the train.

Bert Ward

Below: A Shay of the Wheeler Lumber Company crosses a trestle near Timber, Oregon, amidst the desolation left in the wake of a forest fire.

Top: Small coal burning Shay at work in Coos County. The flat cars have been supplied by the Coos Bay, Roseburg and Eastern, now the Southern Pacific line south from Coos Bay.

G. B. Abdill

Middle: A big load of logs at the Milton Creek Logging Company's dump at St. Helens. The load was 17 feet high.

Bottom: Early log dump of the Eufaula Company on the site of the original dump of Brock's Mosquito and Coal Creek Railroad on Coal Creek Slough.

Willis Gulker

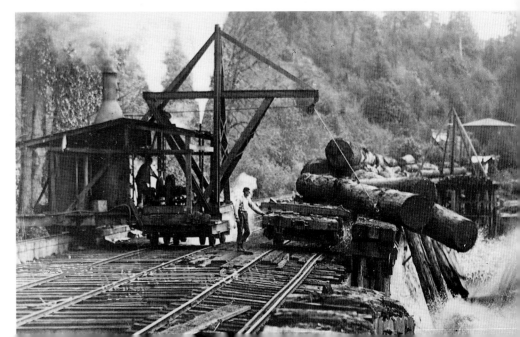

Inclines

One of the most impressive devices used by the loggers was the incline. As the rails worked their way back along the creek bottoms they inevitably reached a point where the abrupt rise of the mountains stalled their progress. Many times a series of switchbacks would get the tracks out on top once more, providing in the process a means of reaching the timber along the face of the mountain. But more often the logger's first need was to get on top with the least waste of time and money; and once on top, his donkey engines could scour the slopes below without trouble.

The shortest distance between two points is still a straight line, and this was the route favored by the loggers—straight up the side of the mountain. Rails were laid for thousands of feet on grades that sometimes surpassed 70 per cent. "Counting the ties" on one of these roads was more like climbing a ladder.

Special donkey engines were built for service on the inclines. They spooled enough line to haul cars and equipment from the bottom to the top, and they had a system of brakes designed to make the handling of heavy loads as safe as possible. Some inclines employed a block car to reduce the strain on the line. This was a large block mounted on a small steel car that was coupled on ahead of the loads. The line passed from the donkey drum down through the block and then back to a tailhold at the top of the incline. Thus, the block cut the pull on the line in half, although it doubled the amount of line needed.

Dangling at the end of this long rope, crews and cars, and even locomotives—all the equipment for the logging camps—were quickly hoisted many hundreds of feet to new locations. Not infrequently, incline would follow incline, so that some operations were carried on at various levels, not unlike the levels in a mine. Nor was it uncommon to find that, once the summit was reached, new inclines were needed to drop down the other side. Cars might be carried up one incline only to be lowered down the next one.

Inevitably there were spectacular wrecks from time to time, when a loaded car would break away and go plunging down to destruction. But they were few and far between, and the loggers took plenty of precautions against accidents. There was always a switch at the bottom of the hill set to deflect a runaway car to a point where a minimum of damage would occur. And, while members of the crew had to be carried up the incline on occasion, riding any type of equipment was discouraged. A runaway down an incline could be a pretty awe-inspiring sight.

Opposite page: Looking up the Porter Carson incline at Estacada, Oregon. Inclines of this type, employing a double track and counterbalanced arrangement, were seldom found in the woods. Distance to the top was 2,700 feet.

Left: A fine example of a switchback in use in the woods. As a general rule, loggers much preferred the incline in a situation of this kind. Lamoine Lumber & Trading Company employed this device to climb out of the Sacramento River Canyon below Dunsmuir, California.

W. B. Fowler

Below: Lifting itself by its bootstraps. This incline donkey is taking itself to the top of the hill where it will be set up to handle the loads of logs. Scene is on the incline of the Porter Carson Logging Company, near Estacada, Oregon—later operated by La Dee Logging Company. Maximum grade here was 50 per cent.

Above: View looking down the Yeon and Pelton incline. The logs had to be worked from the dump down through the tortuous windings of the little slough to a point where the river boats could get a line on them.
J. F. Ford photo from John Yeon's album, courtesy J. Brady

Left: Yeon and Pelton incline machine. Note the heavy brakes for handling the loaded cars on the steep grade. This machine was capable of lowering three loaded cars at a time. It replaced an older machine that handled only two cars.

J. F. Ford photo from John Yeon's album, courtesy J. Brady

Below: Two loads nearing the foot of the incline.

J. F. Ford photo from John Yeon's album, courtesy J. Brady

Right: The shortest distance between two points is a straight line, and many a logger found it the best way to get up and down a hill. This incline of the Wisconsin Logging & Timber Company above Oak Point on the lower Columbia River had a grade of 66 per cent and is fairly typical of inclines all over the West. It was one of a series of inclines used by Wisconsin to get out on top. Cars were raised and lowered on the end of a long line by a heavy incline donkey mounted at the top of the grade.

C. Kinsey photo from the Labbe and Goe collection

Below: Letting a load down the incline of The Whitney Company, up the Kilches River from Idaville, Oregon.

G. B. Abdill

Above: Scene at the head of the Ebey Logging Company incline near Arlington, Washington in 1921 showing the incline donkey and a block car. The block car was used occasionally in later years to give added power and better control on the hill.

Opposite page: Another view of the block car showing how it was used on the incline. Note the line from the donkey passing through the block and back up the hill to the tailhold. Loads are switched out of the siding at the left with the car.

Above: Landing rigged for crotch line loading.

Prentiss photo from John T. Labbe

Left: Over she goes! Another load of logs heads down the Whitney incline.

G. B. Abdill

Below: Head of The Whitney Company incline. The building at left houses the incline donkey, and the tower provides the proper lead for the cables that lower the loaded cars. The three-truck Climax, "Molly-O," is switching some loads into position. Empties on the right-hand track have just come up the incline.

G. B. Abdill

Left: Not all the railroads needed locomotives. Here is a gravity railroad operated like an incline by the Willard Case Lumber Co. The car is hauled up the hill to the landing by a donkey, and lowered again when loaded. The man with the peavey on top of the load would rate a good calling down from present-day safety engineers. Site of the old mill is now within the city limits of Rainier, Oregon.

Tom Timony

Below: Reverse incline on Milton Creek Logging operation. With one landing in a deep hole, the easiest way out was to pull the loaded cars up to the railroad with an incline donkey, a fairly common practice.

Opposite page: A Wheeler Lumber Company Shay is switching a landing near Timber, Oregon, on a frosty winter morning.

Above and below: This brake hickey is designed for use with a brake wheel. Hickey is thrust between the spokes of the wheel and hooked over the shaft to provide added leverage in applying the brakes.

John T. Labbe

Hickeys and Hoggers

The head brakeman was the most important member of the train crew. He determined how the trains were to be made up and laid out the work for the train crew. He also formulated the strategy for controlling the loaded trains on the heavy grades; and where some method of dispatching was employed, it was he who maintained contact with the dispatcher.

The "hickey" was the badge of the brakeman. It was a short iron bar designed to be inserted through the spokes of a brake wheel to provide leverage in tightening up the brake. Manipulation of the brakes on the disconnected trucks was a highly specialized art. They had to be set by hand at the top of the grade, and they often required attention during the descent. If the train was moving slowly he could hop off the footboards of one load and catch the next "hole" as it came by; but if the train was moving too fast, or if he had to make his way forward, he must walk the swaying logs like a circus performer.

The head brakeman had to plan his many complicated switching moves with a minimum of available trackage, and once the landing was switched, he had to rearrange his train to make sure that the most secure loads were in the lead. Nothing but gravity held the cars together, and in a long train there was a tendency for the loads to pull apart. The head brakeman must look them over and determine their stability, and must consider just how much braking power he might apply without pulling them apart. Once his train was made up and he was headed down the hill, he tried to balance his braking so that the locomotive must exert a small effort to keep the cars rolling downhill—and yet, his brakes must not cause the wheels to slide.

The engineer held a position of importance almost equal to that of the head brakeman. He not only ran his locomotive, he was also required to service and maintain it. The engineer's job began an hour or two before the train crews arrived, and many of his weekends and holidays were taken up with such servicing chores as washing the boiler. Very often no fireman was employed and the engineer had the entire responsibility for the engine. However, once on the road one of the brakemen usually took over the firing duties when he was free. As a result of this arrangement, it became common practice for trainmen to move up to engine service as openings developed.

The skill of the engineer with his throttle and brake had to match that of the brakemen with their hickeys. Because of the fragile nature of the cars they handled, they had to be treated gently. Careful starts and smooth stops were second nature to the engineer who handled disconnects; and in later years, when the logging lines began to fade and many of the men drifted on to mainline jobs, they earned an enviable reputation for their skill with the unfamiliar automatic air.

Inevitably, there were engineers who considered themselves to be the most important member of the crew, and who tried to take charge. They might get away with it—until the day they came up against an experienced brakeman. More than one obstreperous engineer has been "given a ride" by his brakemen. With consummate skill the brakie could let the train roll on a grade until it was far past the engineer's ability to cope with it—and then, at the last minute, he could bring it back under control. One or two such experience usually sufficed to mellow the most intractable character, although there were some who required a periodic reminder.

On the other hand, an engineer could make it rough for the brakemen, too. He could do some pretty fast running that crowded the brakies' ability to catch the moving footboards or ride the swaying loads.

Most engineers preferred to keep their engines headed up the hill. This made it easier to keep the crownsheet of the boiler covered with water, and many of them felt that it kept hotter steam in the steam dome. It also allowed them to keep an eye on their trains during the most important period of activity.

The engine was always run on the lower end of the train in descending the hill to guard against the chance of a car breaking loose and plunging down the hill. Some of the early operators had kept their little engines above the train, in the hopes that they could cut loose and save the engine in case of trouble, it being the most valuable piece of equipment on the job. But once the railroads had grown to the point where more than one crew was at work, it became more important to avoid any danger to the other men and equipment.

In climbing the hill the order was reversed. The empty sets of trucks were trailed behind the lokey. When pushed ahead of the engine they had a tendency to bunch up and turn sideways, much as the links of a chain might. It made them hard to shove and difficult to keep on the rail. Trailing out behind they rolled freely and easily.

To guard against the chance of the trucks getting away on the upgrade, the brakies rode them-spacing themselves at intervals. And it was the usual practice to jam a board or limb into the last drawhead, so that any crew member could tell at a glance that the train was still intact.

Below: This is the way the brakes are handled on the disconnected trucks. The iron hickey is hooked into the brake wheel and the tension adjusted according to the requirements of the situation. Two trucks can be handled from each "hole." Here a Crown-Zellerbach loader is letting a couple of loads roll free of the landing to make room for more cars.

Right: The brakeman here holds a "hickey" designed for use with the vertical brake staff used on some types of disconnected trucks. The end of the staff was squared and the socket in the hickey fit over it.

C. Kinsey photo from Rudy Larson

Below: Truck equipped with a vertical brake stand. Hickey is fitted to the squared top of the shaft.

Mrs. J. F. Blair

Above: The brakeman keeps an eye on his train as it descends a grade on the line of the C. D. Johnson Lumber Company between Siletz and Toledo, Oregon.
B. H. Ward

Below: Oregon-American's No. 106 pulls up to the water tank with a string of empties. Note the brakemen riding the trucks and the stick propped up on the last truck. This stick was known as a telltale, and its presence indicated at a glance that the train was still intact.

Right: Note the wooden block bolted to the truck of this fire car which served as a step for the brakeman. Steps such as this were fairly common in the woods. They gave better footing for the brakeman in his calked boots than did the usual iron step.

Below: The Silver Falls Timber Co. 2-spot and a train of loaded log flats high in the hills east of Silverton. This was one of the few Oregon lines to have a snow problem in winter. There were times when camps were snowbound and equipment was stalled in huge drifts despite the efforts of men and snow plows.

Drake photo from the Oregon Historical Society

Left: Crown-Willamette Paper Company No. 5. This little 2-6-2T came from Rainier, Oregon, where it had been working for Hammond Lumber Company. In June of 1928, Crown-Willamette became Crown-Zellerbach.

Below: Crown-Zellerbach tank Mallet No. 12 switches the landing at the reload. Loaded cars are dropped into the hole by gravity, and before heading back the loads must be rearranged to put the solidest cars in the lead, lest they pull apart on the way out.

Above: Sunset Logging Company's No. 25 after she got away on a hill. The regular engineer was off and the "donkey doctor" was taking his place. Sunset used Southern Pacific cars with airbrake equipment, and he started down the hill before remembering to pump up his air. The crew left her and no one was hurt, although the train piled up on top of a watchman's shanty which was occupied. The No. 25 was one of two two-truck Willamettes, coming to Sunset from East Side Logging Company at Keasey. She was rebuilt and went back to work, but was scrapped at Timber, Oregon, when the operation ended. *Ed Peterson*

Below: All in the day's work on a logging railroad. This scene is on the line of the Silverton Lumber Company. *Drake photo from the Oregon Historical Society*

Above: Eastern and Western Lumber Company's 2-spot on the way to the dump on Coal Creek Slough from Eufaula. Eastern and Western and Benson Logging Company were the two diehard users of link and pin couplers. Much to the distress of the safety engineers, they clung to them until the end. Note the dual gauge track. The original narrow gauge line at Eufaula was continued until the area it served was cut out.

Miller-Freeman Publications

Couplers and Roosters

In the beginning the loggers used link and pin couplers. They had been the accepted practice for years on the railroads, and at about the time the loggers turned generally to railroading the knuckle coupler was coming into common usage, thereby making much link and pin equipment available at salvage prices. But the link and pin had many advantages for loggers. They were less complicated, and thus easier to maintain; and most of their components could be fabricated in the camp shops. Furthermore, by substituting a longer bar for the link, they could be adapted to the ungainly loads with their long overhanging logs.

Inevitably, however, the knuckle coupler found its way into the woods, despite the several handicaps involved. To overcome some of them the loggers adopted an extended knuckle. There was no standard coupler height employed in the woods. Some operators preferred to use a low coupler to give greater clearance to knots and limbs. Others used a high coupler on the footboard end of the truck, but a low coupler under the loads. Still others used a coupler of standard height straight through. In time this equipment was all mixed up, and many operators found themselves with a large variety of couplers. The extended knuckle enabled all these types to be coupled together with a reasonable expectation of reliable operation. The locomotives made use of a drawhead that could be positioned in several slots with a minimum of effort, and thus could be brought into position for the car to be coupled.

But no coupler could equal the link and pin in reliability against uncoupling unexpectedly. Oftentimes the track was so rough that the couplers could slip apart as the cars crossed over dips in the track. This situation was aggravated when the couplers differed radically in height. Thus it became common practice for the crew cars to be fastened with a safety chain or strap, in addition to the coupler, and a brakie always rode where he could take charge of the hand wheel in an emergency. Straps were also used to pick up cars shunted into temporary sidings, such as those used to store the crew cars during the day.

One concession made to the versatility of the old link and pin was a slot in the center of the knuckle. The knuckle was drilled so that a pin could be dropped in to hold a link in the slot. This allowed them to use both types of equipment in the same trains; and it also allowed the use of a long bar in lieu of the link. Now they could couple two trucks together with the bar, or "rooster" as it was called, when the weight of the load might be insufficient to hold them together. Loads could be coupled some distance apart when it was necessary to give clearance to a long overhang. In the end, the ingenious logger made the switch to knuckle couplers without giving up any of the advantages of the old link and pins.

Above: This is the face of a working logging engine. She is Oregon-American No. 104, a Baldwin side tanker. Note the pump on the running board, which was used for everything from transferring fuel to fighting fire. Piled on the front deck are blocks, line, chain, rerailing frogs and an assortment of tools. Draped over the number plate is a strap to be used as an added safety precaution when coupled to the crew car. The front coupler has an extended knuckle, complete with a slot that can be adapted to link and pins, extension bars or the eye of a strap.

Below: Homemade Oregon-American crew car. The nameplate on the end of the car has been salvaged from a Willamette donkey. The coupler has been lowered for mating with the disconnected trucks.

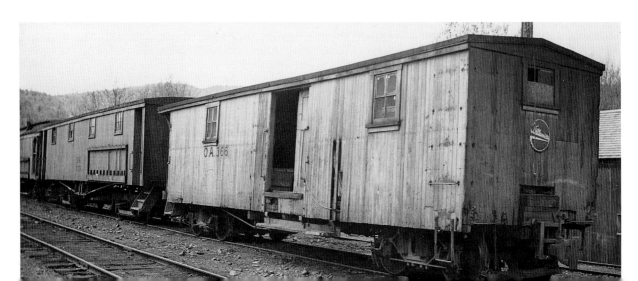

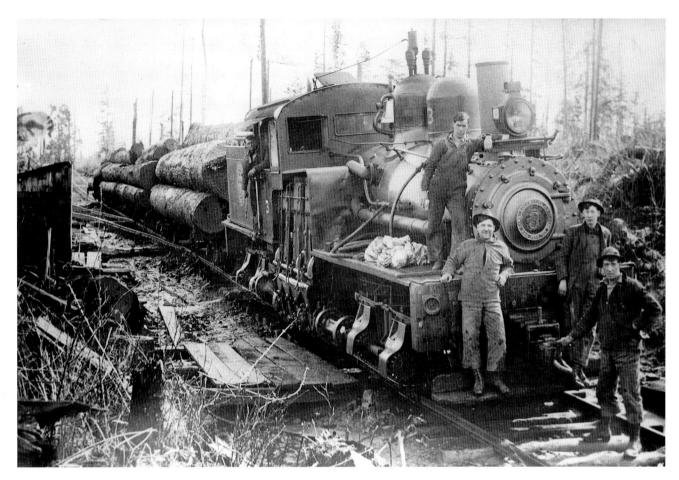

Above: Cathlamet Timber Company's No. 3 was built by Lima in 1909. The front coupler is a knuckle-type, but it carries an old style link in the slotted knuckle.
H. S. Turley

Bottom left: A link and pin coupled to a knuckle coupler, although in this instance the knuckle has been removed for the purpose. These cars are on the narrow gauge line of the West Side Lumber Company at Tuolumne, California.
H. J. Vanderveen

Bottom middle: Photo showing the adaptability made possible by the use of the extended knuckle. These couplers are on two of the crew cars of the Oregon-American Lumber Company. Oregon-American used disconnnects with low couplers, while their other equipment was standard. Note that the coupler on the right is capable of being lowered to match the disconnnects. Car on the left is No. 370, a homemade crew car using passenger trucks which set it higher than the rest. This car extended too far over the coupler and once crushed a brakeman on the footboards of a tank engine in coupling.

Bottom right: Coupled—thanks to extended knuckles.

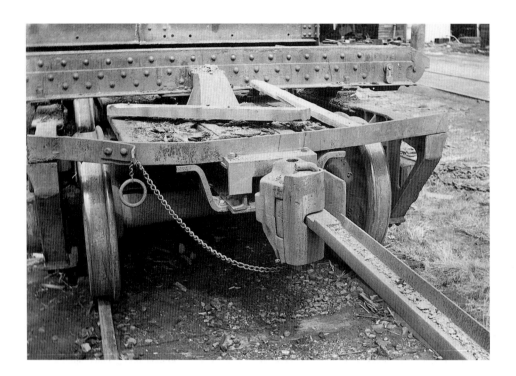

Above and below: Rooster is coupled into slot on regular knuckle and held in place by the pin dropped down through a hole in the knuckle. This gave great versatility to the standard coupler, allowing it to couple with link and pin equipment, and also making it possible to hook chains or cable for a pull. Roosters were used to hold trucks together, to make up a car or for holding light loads together, and they were also used to give added clearance between cars with long overhanging loads.

Above: Two Shays of the Chapman Timber Company, of Scappoose, Oregon, struggle up a 12 per cent grade with a steam donkey. The equipment uses knuckle couplers, but roosters are used for clearance.

B. H. Ward

Below: Palmer Libby train at Blind Slough. Note that the trucks under the first car are tied together with chain, a practice often employed when the load appeared in danger of pulling apart.

Mrs. J. F. Blair

Above: A load of beautiful old growth piling moves out of the woods. The disconnected trucks could handle unbelievably awkward loads. The logs might drag along the rails and bend around steep banks on the curves, but seldom did this action derail the trucks.

Prentiss Photo from the Collection of Labbe and Goe

Special Equipment

The loggers developed a great deal of specialized equipment for use on their rails. Much of it came to be more or less "standard" for such lines. All of it was developed right on the job out of necessity and need.

The disconnected logging truck was one of the more distinctive items. It was versatile and light and functional. It could be adapted to logs of 16 feet or 80 feet with equal ease. It was easy to build and maintain, and it was light enough for the engines to boost back up the heavy grades.

Another was the crew car. Known also as the "crummy," or "mulligan car," this car was designed to get the loggers out on the job in the morning and to bring them back at night. It had no standard style or appearance, being just what was at hand, or what could be fixed up for the comfort of the men. Many times it consisted of an open flatcar with longitudinal seats. Sometimes a roof was added for protection in wet weather. Or it may have been built up out of an old boxcar and contain the luxury of a stove. Finally in the Twenties, when the interurbans began to fade from the scene, they showed up on many logging lines. Built for use on sharp curves, they were ideally suited to the roads the loggers used. And, while the cars held together under such rough treatment, and the logger's caulked boots, the men rode in style.

The moving car became such an important item of equipment it was soon commercially available from several manufacturers. Essentially a heavy duty flatcar, it was modified to suit the needs of the logger. It was used for moving donkey engines, buildings on skids, caterpillar-style tractors, trucks or anything else that could conceivably be handled on a flat car. The donkeys were loaded on their huge skids under their own power, and so the car had to have a smooth steel deck with rounded edges to prevent hangups, and the brake levers were mounted below the level of the deck. Most of these cars were a variant on the standard heavy duty flatcar, but some of them were built up with heavy girder frames and double sets of trucks. Several engines could make hard work of handling such a car loaded with a big steam donkey.

Camp cars were used by many of the companies whose ever expanding lines required periodic moves. These cars were built by the companies and were normally too large to move over a standard railroad. Often being as much as 16 feet wide and 60 feet or more in length, these cars carried all the necessary functions of the camp. There were bunk cars, mess cars, commissary cars, office cars, shop cars, a car for the saw filer—and sometimes even a post office and movie theatre. As a rule, the bachelor camp was composed of small cabins mounted on runners, and these were slipped aboard the moving cars for the move. The trucks and hardware used in these cars was composed of discarded equipment picked up from the scrap yards, and in later days much of it bore inscriptions and dates to awe the inquiring railfan.

Gasoline motor cars were used in the woods for years. Some of the early ones were rebuilt from old automobiles for the use of officials or section crews. Some were rebuilt into crew cars. A little later some of the coach builders began to turn out various types of busses, or rail cars, for use on lightly traveled lines—and the loggers found them useful. Before long the big crew speeders became a standard piece of logging equipment. Many of them were built in company shops, but many more were turned out by commercial builders.

Most impressive of all the machines used in the woods was the skidder. This was a huge, rail mounted logging engine. In one unit, it combined both yarding and loading donkeys supplied by a single boiler. In its final stage, the skidder carried its own steel tower, in lieu of a spar tree. These goliaths weighed from 300 to 400 tons, and they were carried on multiple trucks. Even so, the weight on the track was brutal—especially when it is considered that these machines were taken into an operation over green fills and freshly excavated cuts. And normally these logging spurs were laid with light rail and little ballast. It took a battery of geared locomotives, all working their hearts out in unison, to work a skidder back into the hills. And more than one of them, finding a soft spot in the grade, toppled down into the canyon. But the loggers always managed to fish them out again and get them back on their way up the hill.

Most of these big machines were built by Lidgerwood, or under their license. However, there were a few others built. Willamette Iron and Steel Company built a number of tree rigged skidders. They also built one tower skidder, a 300-ton machine with a 100 foot steel tower, for Crown-Willamette Paper Company, at Cathlamet. Washington Iron Works put out some skidders for Long-Bell, at Ryderwood, that were powered by electricity. Long power cables followed them about the operation carrying power generated at the mill in Longview. Long-Bell also had a huge diesel powered skidder that weighed 400 tons, reputedly the heaviest skidder used. And just like the others, this one managed to topple down the hillside, taxing the ingenuity of the men who had to salvage it.

Below: The Whitney Company's "Siwash" with a big stick to be dumped into Blind Slough. This was the "world's tallest flagpole," a gift from the city of Astoria to the Pan Pacific Exposition in San Francisco. The top of the pole stood 230 feet above the ground.

Ray Davis

Right: Coast Range Lumber Company No. 15, operating in the hills northeast of Eugene, Oregon, was once a steam dummy. The open air crew car has been built up by adding a deck to a pair of disconnected trucks. Coast Range was a subsidiary of the Portland Lumber Company.

M. F. Whitbeck

Below: Headed for work on a rainy Oregon morning. The crew of the brand new Spaulding Miami Lumber Company operation at Grand Ronde, Oregon, rides on an improvised crew car behind a badly overloaded Model T Ford on this November day in 1921.

University of Oregon collection

Left and below: This old interurban car was built in 1908 for the brand new Oregon Electric Railway, and when the OE gave up its electric passenger service the old combine came to the woods as a crew car. Before it came to Oregon-American it was used by Consolidated Timber Company for many years. Car was 49 years old when this picture was taken and was scrapped soon after when the operation ended.

Above: Long-Bell No. 102 handles the crew car. This little Shay was the "bullcook" engine for Oregon-American and Long-Bell at Vernonia. She was once the 2-spot on the line of Western Cooperage at Olney and now stands proudly on display in the center of Vernonia, Oregon.
Gregory Kamholz

Below: Crew car built by the Oregon-American Lumber Company for their operation in the hills west of Vernonia. Rack on the side was for carrying axes and other tools. Saw racks were usually hung under the frame in the center of the car. Note the old passenger car trucks, quite a luxury in the woods.

Top: Moving car of the Western Lumber Company, at West Fir, Oregon. Doesn't look as though that hand brake is very serviceable, but the photo was taken in 1954 when the line was being torn up.

Middle: Heavy duty moving car as used by many of the logging roads. This one has just brought a donkey down to Keasey from the Oregon-American operation.

Bottom: The camp of Holland, Briggs and Avery nestles in a canyon at the edge of Grays River Valley. It is fairly typical of the small camps that sprang up like mushrooms in the Northwest woods.

Photo from Ernest Strom—courtesy of the Wahkiakum County Museum

Above: Retired Rayonier camp cars at Railroad Camp, near Hoquiam, Washington.

Below: Building camp cars at Camp No. 3 of the Big Creek Logging Company out of Knappa, Oregon.

C. Kinsey photo—Labbe and Goe collection

Left: Small camp car built on a single truck from a little dump car. This was the home of the blacksmith at Oregon-American's Camp McGregor. Once when the camp was moved they left the car behind—on purpose-but the next Sunday the blacksmith went down and put it on the track himself, and the first crew through on Monday found it on the mainline. After that, it accompanied the rest of the buildings.

Right: Truck under a Rayonier camp car. This was an old Northern Pacific truck as indicated by the initials impressed in the wooden cross beam of the bolster. When the photo was taken in 1955, the truck was probably sixty years old.

Left: Small camp car still in use by Rayonier, Inc. at Railroad Camp, north of Hoquiam, Washington.

Above: Camp cars at Camp McGregor of the International Paper Company, formerly the Oregon-American Lumber Company, west of Vernonia. Camp McGregor was burned out in the great Tillamook fire, but was rebuilt and lasted for many years while the burned timber was salvaged. The picture was taken in March of 1957, near the end of the operations.

Below: Interior of a Big Creek camp car, showing how roomy and comfortable such cars could be. The mess hall is typical of most of those found in logging camps. Poster on the left wall encourages enlistment in the First World War, while those around the rear promote Liberty Bonds.

Weister Co. photo—from Willard Evenson

Top: Mike Kaufmann, superintendent of Deer Island Logging Company aboard the speeder for the trip to the woods northwest of St. Helens, Oregon.

Middle: Oregon-American's No. 10 speeder. This unit was designed primarily for handling supplies and mail.

Below: A Long-Bell speeder takes some of the brass for an inspection trip in the woods above Ryderwood, Washington.

J. M. McClelland, Jr.

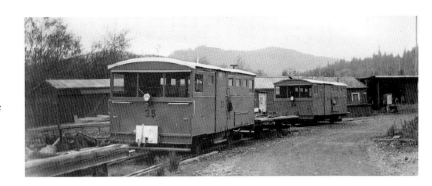

Top: Crew speeders at Camp Hoko on the Clallam operations of Rayonier, Inc.

Middle: These Crown-Zellerbach speeders at Cathlamet were built by the Skagit Steel and Iron Works of Sedro Woolley, Washington.

Below: Oregon-American's No. 11 speeder. She carried the mail and supplies from Keasey up to camp. Powered with a diesel engine, she was also capable of handling a couple of loaded cars. Now and then she was used to haul the crew cars or oil cars.

Randolph Brandt

Above: Brooks-Scanlon Lumber Company loading cars with a McGiffert Loader. Note the horses and the set of High Wheels that have yarded the logs to the landing. This was in the pine country south of Bend, Oregon.

Miller-Freeman Publications

Below: Loading pine in Eastern Oregon on the Pelican Bay Lumber Company's operation north of Klamath Falls. The loader straddled the track and the empties passed beneath it, an arrangement much favored in the pine country.

Jack Holst

Right: The tower skidder was the most monstrous logging machine used in the woods. Weighing hundreds of tons and mounted on railroad trucks, they were taken up heavy grades and over soft trackage in defiance of all physical laws. This view on the Washington Pulp and Paper Company operation near Neah Bay at the northwest tip of the Washington peninsula shows the tower folded in moving position.

Timber Views Company photo from Ed Stamm

Below: The crew train makes a stop at a skidder side in the late afternoon. The big tower on the Lidgerwood dwarfs the little train. Scene is on the Washington Pulp and Paper Corporation operation at Neah Bay.

Timber Views Company photo from E. P. Stamm

Opposite above: Willamette donkeys loaded aboard disconnects for the trip to the woods. This method of transporting donkeys was not unusual practice. Scene was the Whitney Company operation at Idaville, Oregon.

Opposite below: Crown-Willamette Paper Company bought the only tower skidder built by Willamette Iron and Steel Company and put it to work on the Elochoman (also spelled as Elokomin) back of Cathlamet. She carried a steel tower a hundred feet tall, and she weighed around three hundred tons. She was scrapped some time in 1959.

Below: Willamette tower skidder at work for Crown-Willamette Paper Company near Cathlamet. The operator of a donkey engine was commonly called a "donkey puncher," but on a skidder he was known as the "leverman."

Left: Three locomotives couple into a Clark and Wilson skidder preparatory to moving her out.

C. Kinsey photo from Charlie Smith

Below: Tree-rigged electric skidder used by Long-Bell Lumber Company on their operation at Ryderwood. High tension cables had to be strung behind these machines to provide the power from the powerhouse at the mill.

Prentiss photo from the Labbe and Goe collection

Above: At least once in each setting a skidder had to be turned around. Half the circle was logged from one side of the spar tree, and then the skidder was swung around to the other side of the tree to get the rest of the circle. There were no turntables and few wye tracks, but the resourceful loggers didn't need them. They pushed the skidder up two diverging tracks, as shown here, until it was at right angles to the locomotive. Then they moved over and coupled onto the other end and pulled it back. This scene is at Big Creek.
George Morrice

Below: Unloading device developed by Benson to handle the unusually long loads for which the operation was famous.
Miller-Freeman Publications

Left: One style of jillpoke used for unloading. This one was used at Sekiu, on the Strait of Juan de Fuca, by Rayonier. Several arms, like spokes of a wheel, radiate from the center axis. As the cars pass by, the spokes turn, shoving the logs into the water. Note how the inner rail is raised to help tip the logs off the cars.

Below: Jillpoke used by the Wisconsin Logging and Lumber Company. The end of the beam was placed against the load, and as the train moved ahead it swung around, forcing the logs off the car.
University of Oregon Collection

Top: Deep River Logging Company train. The tiny crummy is built on a single disconnected truck. In a train of loaded cars it was carried next to the tender.

S. B. Lawrence

Middle: Rayonier caboose painted bright green and yellow. Two of these see service on the Clallam line out of Sekiu. Photo was taken at Camp Hoko.

Below: Small caboose used by Crown-Zellerbach train crews at Cathlamet.

Above: An important part of railroad logging in later years was the fire car; old tank cars to carry water and equipped with auxiliary pump and hose lines. These cars belonged to Crown-Zellerbach, at Cathlamet.

Below: Steam from the locomotive boiler was put to many uses. Here Crown-Zellerbach is using it to transfer diesel fuel for the trucks from the tank car to a nearby storage tank. Most tank cars used in the woods had a small steam pump mounted on them for such purposes, or for use in fire fighting.

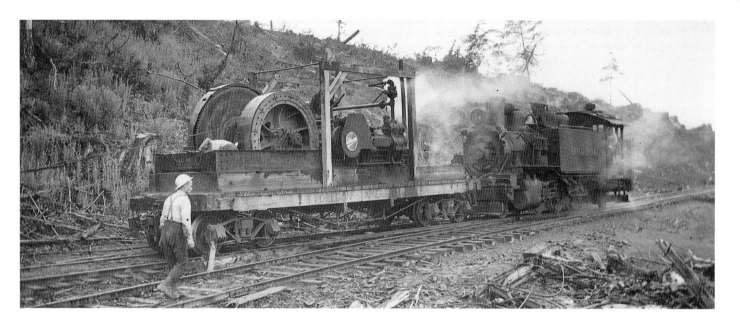

Above: Gathering up line at the Long-Bell show out of Vernonia. An old incline drum is mounted on a flatcar and powered with steam from the locomotive.

Below: A couple of big fir logs move out of Eastern and Western's Eufaula operation behind a Shay. Just ahead of the engine is a set of loading drums mounted on a car. Steam from the locomotive is used to operate the drums in loading.

J. F. Ford photo from Miller-Freeman Publications

Top: A Crown-Willamette Paper Company experiment. Utilizing a five-ton truck drive and a 100-horse-power Hercules motor, this gasoline locomotive was an attempt to put the trucks on rails. It was never a threat to the steam engines.

Mr. Duggan

Middle: Tracklaying machine known as a "Japanese Skidder" at Camp McGregor of Oregon-American. Railroad loggers were constantly pulling up track and relaying it in new location, which made such machines a valuable asset.

Bottom: Loading ballast cars at Silver Falls Timber Company.

Drake photo from Oregon Historical Society

Above: Rotary snowplow used by Long-Bell on their California operation at Tennant.

B. H. Ward

Below: Rotary snowplows were rare in the woods, most loggers preferring to settle for a wedge plow attached to the front of a locomotive. This little plow was used on the three-foot gauge line of the Swayne Lumber Company of Oroville, California.

B. H. Ward

Above: A logging camp of the Spruce Division. These temporary Army camps were later replaced by more permanent camps with wooden buildings.

University of Oregon—Oregon Collection

Spruce Division

The First World War presented the lumber industry with a peculiar challenge. Suddenly the armies of the world were taking wings. The Germans were pressing hard along the Marne, and farsighted officers recognized that the future, in all probability, lay with the airplane. Overnight the demand for spruce lumber of airplane quality became paramount, and in the spring of 1917 the United States Government set out to acquire large quantities of it.

The spruce had never been considered a valuable or desirable tree for lumber, and few logging operations were able to tap stands of spruce in abundance. Most of the great stands of spruce were along the western slope of the Coast Range where the loggers had found little cause to build their lines.

By the fall of 1917 the government was receiving but three million feet of spruce a month, and only a small part of the three million feet was of airplane quality. Colonel Disque, later to become General Disque, was sent out in October to take charge of the program and to increase both the quality and the quantity of production. Ten million feet a month was needed—and all of top quality.

Arriving in Portland on October 11, 1917, Colonel Disque went immediately into a huddle with the leaders in the lumber industry. As a result of what he learned, it was apparent that the industry was not capable of meeting the requirements through normal trade channels. Colonel Disque returned to the East to make his report and received a green light for his plan to set up the Spruce Production Division.

As soon as possible, the spruce forests were cruised and bought by the government. Loggers from whistle punk to top executive were inducted into the Army and put to work in the woods at the jobs they knew best. A cut-up, or remanufacturing, plant was set up in Vancouver, Washington, to handle the output of the mills. As fast as the spruce could be harvested it found its way to the existing sawmills, where it was broken down into cants for the final finishing in the specialized cut-up plant.

To get into the areas where the spruce grew required new railroads, and under government sponsorship some 13 were laid out. Nine of these were of a temporary character, but four of them were designed as permanent railroads. One of these was the Clallam County Railroad, later becoming the Port Angeles Western, at the northern tip of the Olympic Peninsula. The other Washington line was along the north bank of the Nemah River on Willapa Bay.

There were two other permanent railroads located in Oregon, both of them contingent to Yaquina Bay. One of them was known as the Yaquina Northern. It left the Southern Pacific mainline at Yaquina and followed around the north shore of the bay, eventually heading up the coast to Otter Rock. The other line was known as the Alsea Southern. It had no physical connection with any other line, but began at the log dump near South Beach and headed south almost to Yachats, crossing Alsea Bay on a long trestle.

The other nine lines were considered temporary in character. First, at the north end of the Olympic Peninsula, was a spur track constructed by Merrill and Ring and operated in conjunction with their own operation. Further south, below Lake Quinault, was another similar spur built off the Polson Logging Company's line. In Grays Harbor County, near the town of Westport, was the Elk River Railroad, and across the Nemah River, in Pacific County, was another along the south bank of the river. A little further south along the Naselle River was the last of the Washington lines, a three-foot gauge road about two miles long.

Continuing south through Oregon, the site of the first line was in Clatsop County. A narrow gauge line was projected along the Lewis and Clark River, but was abandoned. However, a standard gauge line 13 miles in length was built up the Lewis and Clark River from a junction with the SP&S at Clatsop. The next temporary line was called the Toledo and Siletz Railroad, or No. 10. Oddly enough, this was the last of the 13 lines to see service, being abandoned on the last day of 1959. It outlasted all the "permanent" railroads. And last of the 13 lines on the Spruce Division was a mile and a half of trackage out of Beaverhill, in Coos County.

In its urgency to get into production on the vital spruce, the government moved ahead without regard to obstacles. Rails were laid first and rights of way acquired later. And to tide things over until production had been achieved, crews went to work felling and splitting the huge spruce trees. Plank roads were laid and the spruce "flitches" were brought out on trucks with solid rubber tires. Logging camps were set up in Army tents, and loggers worked in Army uniforms. Army procedure governed the mess halls and the Army medics supervised sanitary and health conditions.

They brought out the spruce! As time went on and the urgency of the situation increased, the demand for airplane spruce was raised from the original ten million feet to thirty million feet a month-and the loggers got it out. In October 1918, less than a year after the program had been instituted, the cut-up plant in Vancouver put out 28,681,239 feet of spruce, of which 20,282,933 feet was of airplane quality. Undoubtedly, the success of the Spruce Division had a marked effect on the fortunes of the battles along the Marne; and may, indeed, have been a deciding factor.

The seldom told story of the Spruce Division is one altogether fitting for the minions of Paul Bunyan, and it is doubtful if Paul, himself, could have done a better job of it.

Below: A train of heavily loaded cars on the Coats Fordney operation on Grays Harbor. With logs like these, output figures could reach impressive totals for the day.

C. Kinsey photo from George Morrice

Above: No. 6 of the Warren Spruce Company is getting out spruce logs for the Spruce Production Division to help get an Allied air force into the skies over France. The year is 1918 and the loggers are wearing the uniform of the U.S. Army.

University of Oregon Collection

Above: Scene along the Yaquina Northern. After leaving the bay at Newport, the line followed closely along the coast as far as Cape Foulweather.

Below: Coos Bay Lumber Company No. 10 switching a landing near Powers, Oregon.

Above: This little Heisler was rushed to the aid of the Spruce Division, which, in 1918, was building 13 railroads to tap the stand of spruce for Allied airplanes. In less than a year's time, the hard working soldiers of the Spruce Division were turning out nearly 30,000,000 feet of spruce a month.

University of Oregon—Oregon Collections

Left: The Yaquina and Northern shops as they looked in 1935, shortly before being dismantled. When the winter storms blew in from the southwest, piling waves high on the beach, the salt spray came whipping in and the rain beat a tattoo on the sheet iron building—life around the engine house could be pretty miserable. Note the odd little trestle supporting the switch into the building.

Below: "On the ground" the hard way. This rod engine found a soft spot in the dump and now rests on the bottom of Depot Slough, near Toledo, Oregon.

University of Oregon Collection

Right: Lidgerwood tower skidder hard at work for Silver Falls Timber Company. As happened not infrequently, this machine once found a soft spot in a new grade and toppled down the side of a mountain.

Drake photo from the Oregon Historical Society

Below: Wreck of a Shay in Clatsop County, Oregon. This is thought to have been a construction train on one of the Spruce Division railroads.

Mr. Park

Above: The second engine on Brock's railroad at Eufaula was this little Baldwin tanker known as the "Rattler." Brock operated this three-foot gauge railroad for nearly twenty years before selling out to Eastern and Western Lumber Company. The Rattler was acquired in 1890, and she handled the job until 1900, when a Climax took over.

R. H. Gardiner photo from W. W. Brock

The North Bank

No railroad was ever built down the Washington shore of the Columbia below Longview, and yet there is scarcely a section of land between there and the sea that hasn't shuddered to the passing of the log trains. Men, equipment and supplies came in by boat and barge, and the logs were scattered to the scores of mills along the river behind the straining river boats.

The first logging locomotive came to the Columbia area early in 1883. She was the little "Ant," and she came down from the Puget Sound area after many years of service on the three-foot gauge Seattle and Walla Walla railway, and earlier for the Seattle Coal and Transportation Company. She only weighed seven tons, and she wasn't much of a locomotive, but she came to the logging woods already weighted down with history. A little 0-4-0 side tanker with 6 × 12-inch cylinders, she was built by Hinckley & Company, of San Francisco, in their Fulton Iron Works, and was said to be the first narrow-gauge engine built on the Pacific Coast. She made her trial trip on October 13, 1871, after which she was shipped to Seattle. On March 25, 1872 she made her first trip from the foot of Pike Street to the south end of Lake Union with a special party carried in eight coal cars. With the inauguration of service on this little portage line, she is believed to be the first locomotive of any kind to be operated in the Puget Sound area.

By 1883 the little engine had come to the end of its usefulness to its Seattle owners and was sold to Julius Ordway and George W. Weidler, two Portland lumbermen with extensive logging interests in the Columbia basin. The Ant arrived at Kalama on a flatcar, where she was transferred to a barge for the trip down the river to Oak Point. There she was used in the construction of a railroad for Ordway and Weidler. This is believed to have been the line operated by the Benson Logging and Lumber Company. She made her first trip for them on May 5, 1883, becoming thereby the first logging locomotive to operate on the Columbia River.

Meanwhile, a few miles upriver from Oak Point, at Eufaula, B. F. Brock was hard at work on the construction of a logging railroad. Mr. Brock was born and raised in Vermont, where he had worked his way up to an important position in a locomotive shop before deciding to come West. After considering entering the sheep business in Eastern Oregon, he moved to the Lower Columbia where he entered the logging business with his brother. They began logging with bulls along Fall Creek, just west of Eufaula, about 1875.

Ordway and Weidler financed a number of the early loggers, including Simon Benson, and it seems not unlikely that they had a similar arrangement with Brock. At any rate, on the second day of January 1883, Mr. Brock began grading his railroad along Coal Creek from Coal Creek Slough. The line followed up Coal Creek to Mosquito Creek and up Mosquito Creek to the community of Eufaula. It was chartered as the Mosquito and Coal Creek Railroad. In October 1883 Mr. Brock bought the Ant from Ordway and Weidler for $2000 and the Mosquito and Coal Creek Railroad was in business.

The little Ant was retired in 1890 in favor of a Baldwin 0-6-0 saddle tanker of 14 tons, which was known as the "Rattler," and about 1900 the Rattler was replaced by a 28-ton Climax. In 1902 Mr. Brock sold out the entire operation to the Eastern and Western Lumber Company, of Portland. And when he retired to operate a general store at Stella, near where he had begun his logging career, he took the Ant with him and put it on display nearby. Ultimately it was acquired by Long-Bell and moved to Longview where it stood beside the enginehouse for many years. It met its end when unsupervised scrappers cut it up by mistake.

Hard on the heels of the Ant came a steady procession of logging engines. For 76 years they huffed and puffed their way up the steep canyons and along the high ridges. Over the years the miles of rolling hills were stripped bare; and yet, today, if one would seek evidence of Brock's little railroad, he must hunt through the dim depths of a new forest grown to maturity in the years since the Ant left the scene. When Crown-Zellerbach closed down the railroad at Cathlamet in 1959, and the last echo of the steam whistle had died away along the timbered hills, it marked the end of an era that belonged to steam alone.

Below: The Ant is pictured here after her retirement in 1890-before being put on display at Stella. Long-Bell ultimately got her and moved her to Longview, where she was later scrapped.

W. W. Brock

Below: The little Ant pauses at Eufaula for a picture before backing her train down to the river. Built by Hinckley, of San Francisco, in 1871, she was the first narrow-gauge engine built on the West Coast. She was also the first engine to operate on Puget Sound, and when she came to the Columbia River in 1883 she became the first logging engine on the river. B. F. Brock bought her in October 1883 for his Mosquito and Coal Creek Railroad, and he didn't take any chances on losing her in a wreck. He ran his trains with the engine on the upper end.

Cawthorn photo from W. W. Brock

Left: No. 7 of the Wisconsin Logging and Timber Company works the dump at Midway Landing, Washington. Along the rugged north bank of the Columbia it was often hard to find a spot to come down for a dump. The Baldwin Prairie engine sports a pilot on both ends, unusual in the woods. Also unusual was the practice of heading the loco downhill. Usually, the engines were headed uphill to insure plenty of water over the boiler's crownsheet.

Joe Schrieber

Below: B. F. Brock's second engine, a little Baldwin nicknamed the "Rattler," poses in camp at Eufaula.

R. H. Gardiner photo—from W. W. Brock

Above: In 1899 B. F. Brock bought this Climax engine for his Mosquito and Coal Creek Railroad and the days of the little Ant began to seem like ancient history. In 1902 the entire operation was sold to the Eastern and Western Lumber Company and Brock retired to operate his general store at Stella.
W. W. Brock

Below: Scene of Brock's dump on Coal Creek Slough. The Rattler has just arrived with her train from Eufaula.
R. H. Gardiner photo from W. W. Brock

Above: Eastern and Western Lumber Company No. 1, a Baldwin 2-6-2, doubles as a loading donkey in the woods near Eufaula. A line from the drums behind the engine is being used to load the cars. This is not far from the place where the Ant first began hauling logs to the Columbia more than twenty years earlier.

University of Oregon Collection

Above: Ostrander No. 1 at the dump beside the placid Cowlitz River north of Kelso, Wasington. In the background is the Northern Pacific mainline.
J. M. McClelland, Jr.

Below: A pair of early Shays. No. 1 and No. 2 of the Ostrander Railway & Timber Company.
J. M. McClelland, Jr.

Above: An early log train of the Benson Logging and Lumbering Company, near Oak Point, Washington. The logs have been sniped for ground logging, probably by bulls, and the men display the log jacks used for loading and unloading the cars.

Prentiss photo from the University of Oregon Collection

Above: Catastrophe at Eufaula. Eastern and Western piled this one up right in camp. The Shay looks like a total wreck, but someone has salvaged the bell. They used the steam jam for braking at Eufaula, rather than air, and someone let the boiler pressure get too low on a five per cent grade.

Ben Stark

Below: When the pile of logs was cleared away, this is what remained of the Shay. She was rebuilt and put to work in the woods again.

Ben Stark

Above: "Old Rusty," the two-cylinder Shay of the Oak Point Piling and Timber Company, heads for the dump with another trainload of nice logs.

Clyde Lowe

Below: Scene in the camp of the Oak Point Piling and Timber Company in 1907.

E. W. Anderson

Right: The "piling side" of the Oak Point Piling and Timber Company's operation near Oak Point, Washington. Plenty of nice logs on the rollways, but they don't look much like piling. Note the odd vertical cylinders on the little loading donkey.

E. W. Anderson

Below: Two Shays labor mightily to boost a train up an adverse grade. The lead engine is Lima No. 671 that began life as the "Nosey" on the Benson operation at Oak Point. Here she is at work for the Portland Lumber Company near Cathlamet.

H. S. Turley

Left: Mooers' dump at Skamokawa, Washington.

Henry Mooers

Below: Portland Lumber Company's 4-spot pauses in the hills of Wahkiakum County to show off some big timber. The hill in the background has been logged and the slash has been burned, a practice that left utter desolation in its wake. And while these same hills are now covered with a growth of timber, today's loggers are far more foresighted in their logging methods.

Oregon Historical Society

Above: Lima Shay No. 559 of the Benson Logging and Lumbering Company is working along Cameron Creek out of Oak Point on the Washington shore of the Columbia. Benson began building across the river at Clatskanie in 1903 and sold his operation to Wisconsin Logging and Timber Company when he moved. This picture was taken about 1898.
J. F. Ford photo from E. W. Anderson

Below: Portland Lumber Company No. 4 on Grays River. This Shay, and several others owned by Portland, used a straight boiler—an odd arrangement for engines designed to work on steep grades.
Turner A. Pitt photo—Labbe and Goe collection

Above and below: Saldern bought this Climax in 1899 and put it to work on his flimsy trackwork on K-M Mountain above Grays River. As far as Saldern was concerned, it seemed to be a "hard luck" engine. Before very long, the engine was sold to other owners, who, it is to be hoped, had better luck with her.

Both pictures—Mrs. Burns

Above: Engineer F. Stackpool stands beside his engine on an August day in 1900. The little Climax had recently been barged into Grays River for delivery to Saldern.

C. Wirkkala

Below: Three days later, Stackpool was caught in a runaway and died in the wreck.

Wirkkala photo from J. M. McClelland, Jr.

Above: Charlie Bryson makes with the oilcan to please the photographer during a pause in operations at Camp No. 7 of the Big Creek Logging Company near Knappa, Oregon. The big two-truck Shay is a fugitive from the Benson Timber Company at Clatskanie, whose name she still carries on her tank.

Prentiss photo from the Labbe and Goe Collection

The South Bank

The situation along the south bank of the Columbia was somewhat different. In May of 1898, the railroad between Astoria and Portland began service, making the entire territory tributary to the main-line railroads. It facilitated the movement of men, equipment and supplies to the camps along the river. But the logs were still dumped into the waters of the Columbia for delivery to the mills.

As on the Washington shore, the loggers built their railroads into every section of the land, and the results of their labors clogged every creek and slough. The coming of the railroad attracted many sawmills, and the demand for logs kept increasing.

One of the railroads pushing southward toward the Nehalem Valley was destined to become a common carrier of no mean proportions. The Columbia and Nehalem River Railroad left the Columbia River at Kerry and climbed back into the hills along the south bank, crossing the head of OK Creek where the Gripwheel had already made history. Near the top of the hill it entered a tunnel, coming out into the valley of the Nehalem.

Down along the banks of the Fishhawk the main camp was established at Thompson's Siding, and in 1914, in the days just before the outbreak of the First World War, the line was being built down the Fishhawk to the Nehalem. The Kerry interests, who built the line, had their own logging operations; but in addition, they served a number of other large operators. At one time there were more than ten large camps along the line, each with a railroad operation of its own, shipping logs over the "Kerry Line." The little road engines of the Columbia and Nehalem River were working around the clock, day in and day out. Meanwhile, the main shops had been established across the Nehalem below Birkenfeld, and the busy shop crews were hard put to keep ahead of the train crews. This camp was called Camp Neverstill, a title it justly deserved.

The loggers were working on either side of the tunnel and down along the floor of the valley, and before long the rails of the Kerry Line were moving further south into the hills beyond the Nehalem. The rod engines used on the hill had very low drivers, but even so, the trains had to be doubleheaded through the tunnel. A rare sight was a big three truck Climax acting as a helper engine for the rod engines.

Meanwhile, another rail network was working east from Olney on Young's Bay. Variously known as Tidewater Timber Company, Tidewater and Pacific or the Astoria Southern, the line worked over the divide to the Nehalem Valley at Jewell. It never reached the proportions of the Kerry Line, but the Astoria Southern served a number of other operators as a common carrier.

Ultimately, Brix-Woodard built down Buster Creek from Buster Camp on the Kerry Line. As the rails progressed, they approached a spur of the Tidewater operation. And one day a connection was made between the two networks, finally making it possible to start from tidewater at Olney and by devious and tortuous routing reach the interchange at Kerry and a connection with the outside world. Oddly enough, the easiest potential route down the shore of Young's Bay to Astoria never knew a connecting rail link. Equipment was barged in and out from Astoria.

Left: A Benson engine switches a landing above Clatskanie right after an unusual May snowfall. Benson was noted for the length of the loads handled.

C. Kinsey photo

Below: Three nice fir logs standing on SP&S tracks near Portland. Lettering on the trucks indicates that they have come down from the Rock Creek Logging Company over the SP&S, one of the rare instance in which a mainline railroad handled disconnected trucks with hand brakes. They came down from the Vernonia branch and through the tunnel at the head of Cornelius Pass.

Angelus Photo from Labbe and Goe Collection

Above: A Benson Timber Company crew poses atop a load of logs. Such loads were commonplace with Benson.
C. Kinsey photo from Rudy Larson

Below: Simon Benson, drawn by the building boom in Southern California, built a sawmill in San Diego, and in 1906 shipped the first of many seagoing log rafts down the coast from the Columbia River. Logs such as these were used in creating the huge rafts.

Above: This elaborate trestle was employed by the Hammond Lumber Company at Rainier, Oregon, to avoid a grade crossing of the Spokane, Portland and Seattle line.
Willis Gulker

Below: In the great days of logging along the Columbia this scene was repeated in every slough and inlet from the Cascade Mountains to the sea. These are Yeon and Pelton logs being rafted in Rinearson Slough, below Rainier. The river boats were not able to enter the slough because of a low bridge on the Astoria and Columbia River Railroad near its mouth, but they got a line on the raft and pulled it out into the main stream where they could take charge of it.
J. F. Ford photo from Jim Brady

Above: Engine No. 114 of the Columbia & Nehalem River RR. was originally owned by the Northern Pacific Terminal Company which handled the switching chores at the Portland, Oregon, terminal.
H. S. Turley

Below: Coos Bay Lumber Company No. 10 headed for Powers, Oregon, with a train.

Left: Partial view of the dump at Kerry, where the Columbia and Nehalem River dumped the logs from the many camps they served.

M. C. Barhan

Below: One of the "passenger trains" used on the Columbia and Nehalem River Railroad. This one is built up on a White truck chassis.

Above: Spotless Climax of Palmer and Rupp crosses the Nehalem River on a high trestle. Palmer and Rupp logged just below Mist, and their output was handled by the busy engines of the Kerry Line.
Mrs. McPherson

Below: Hard working road engine of the Columbia and Nehalem River Railroad resting at Kerry. No. 117 was one of the Mikes on the "Kerry Line" kept busy around the clock.
Art Johnson

Above: Log train on the Columbia and Nehalem River Railroad headed by engine No. 116.

Art Johnson

Below: An early Shay poses with a train of big spruce and hemlock logs at the dump on Blind Slough. The lokey belonged to Engineer Johnny Hepburn who contracted the hauling for Palmer Libby Logging Company.

Oregon Historical Society

Above and below: Mann and Montgomery (OK Railroad) climbs up out of a canyon above Clifton on the Oregon shore of the Columbia. This company preceded the Oregon Timber and Logging Company operation in this area.

Both pictures—Cecil Bryant

Above: Log train rounding a curve and heading down through Camp No. 9, at Big Creek.

Below: A Sorenson train near Svensen, Oregon, in 1907, after Sorenson had taken over from Masten.

J. G. Kilner

Above: Big Creek's little rod engine went astray. Having a 0-6-0 wheel arrangement, with no pony wheels to steady it, it had a habit of yawing badly on the rough track. She was headed for home with a light train when she managed to hop right off the rail.

Below: Ready to head for the dump with a train of logs on the line of the Big Creek Logging Company at Knappa, Oregon. The engine is Lima No. 2230, recently arrived from the Benson Timber Company at Clatskanie. The fellow in the light shirt is Klews Clauson, head loader. Engineer is Charlie Bryson. And judging by the suitcase and bedroll on the locomotive, someone intends to catch the train at Knappa for the fleshpots of the big city.

University of Oregon Collection

Left: Boomer engine hard at work for the Milton Creek Logging Company near St. Helens, Oregon. Said to be originally from the Pennsy, this little hog came to St. Helens after putting in a stint for Wheeler Lumber Company at Wheeler, Oregon, on Nehalem Bay.

Mrs. Burns

Below: Crown-Willamette Paper Company's No. 4, a three-truck Climax, switches a landing near Cathlamet, Washington. The siding is built on a grade to facilitate switching with the aid of gravity in the absence of the locomotive. Derails are provided to protect the mainline in the event a load should get away. The pipeline beside the rail supplies water to the steam donkeys on the landing.

Above: Palmer and Owens Climax at work in the woods near Youngs Bay.
Ernie Splester

Below: Loading with a hayrack boom on Crown-Willamette Paper Company operation. Trucks are let down into position under the boom by gravity, and once loaded, the car is dropped down to await the arrival of the locomotive.
University of Oregon Collection

Above: Scene on the Beaver Creek Logging Company line near Vernonia. The locomotive is the fourth engine built by the Willamette Iron and Steel Company in Portland. She was delivered to Beaver Creek in April 1923.

Below: Two levels of operations on the line of the Cobbs Mitchell Lumber Company, near Valsetz, Oregon. The Shay-type engine No. 104 on the trestle is the first locomotive built by the Willamette Iron and Steel Works, of Portland. She came to Valsetz from the Coos Bay Lumber Company.

C. Kinsey photo from the Labbe and Goe Collection

Above: Mud Bay Logging Company dump near the head of Puget Sound. The tide is out and the source of the company name is obvious. This was one of the far-flung network of Weyerhaeuser railroads. Mikado No. 4 was turned out for Mud Bay by Baldwin in 1912.
Albert Farrow

Below: Dolbeer and Carson No. 3, a little Prairie type, rumbles out onto a trestle with a train of redwood logs in California's Humboldt County.
Bert Ward

Left: Western Cooperage almost lost the 2-spot in Youngs Bay, near Olney. She got away with a train and came down to the dump out of control. But the loads were ahead of the engine and they piled up high enough to save her. She went from here to Oregon-American, and is now on display in Vernonia.
Clarence Stanley Photo

Below: Palmer Libby log train out of Blind Slough on the lower Columbia. Engineer Floyd Blair is at the throttle. The engine is a Climax, the usual power on Palmer operations after they began operating their own railroads.
Mrs. J. F. Blair

Above: Big Creek's Climax after dropping through a bridge. The bridge was under construction and the train was headed downhill with material for the job when it got away. Everyone scrambled to safety and no one got hurt. The engine was fished out and put back to work again after some rebuilding.

Below: A lazy Sunday afternoon in camp. This is Eastern & Western Lumber Company's Saddle Mountain operation east of Seaside, Oregon.
Mr. Duggan

Above: Small Baldwin saddle tank engine built for Silver Falls Timber Company, of Silverton, Oregon. No. 103 with her sister engine, No. 104, were purchased by the Peninsula Terminal Company of Portland, and they still handle all the switching chores in the North Portland yards.

Rod Engines

The rod engine, as well as the geared engine, has always been a tool of the logger. In the beginning these engines were small tank lokeys that could be easily transported to remote logging sites, although, as has been noted, some larger engines were handed down from the mainline railroads.

The tank engine found much favor with the loggers. It was small and compact, adapting well to the rough and crooked track; and the extra weight of the water and fuel being carried over the boiler added to the weight on the drivers, and thus improved the engine's pulling power. The fact that there was no tender to drag around, or to maintain, was an important factor, also. These features made it practical to operate rod engines on fairly heavy grades, and many of them were bought to work on six and seven per cent. They were used to switch the logging spurs and also served the mainline of the logging roads.

After 1900, these tank engines began to grow in size. For many years the 2-6-2 tank engine was a favorite in the woods, and some of these engines are still in service. In later years these were followed by the larger 2-8-2T and by small tank Mallets.

The 2-6-2 wheel arrangement was also very popular in the tender type engines. These little Prairies carried a large boiler on small wheels, and the short wheelbase made them especially efficient on logging roads, while the pony wheels on either end let them operate forward or backward with equal ease and safety.

By the 1920's many of the logging lines were growing to the proportions of short line railroads. They had logged the timber nearby and had worked their way far back into the hills. Geared engines could no longer operate efficiently on these mainline hauls and the rod engine began to grow in popularity. The Baldwin Locomotive Works dominated this field, manufacturing by far the largest percentage of this type of engine.

Weyerhaeuser Timber Company's many operations constituted the largest network of logging railroads in the world, and they provided the inspiration for many new developments by Baldwin. Following the 2-6-2 engines came the larger 2-8-2 type. These little Mikes proved to be ideal for the larger operations, especially for the mainline haul. Porter turned out a few engines of this type, also, but they failed to find the same favor with the loggers as did the Baldwins.

What was probably the first Mallet designed for logging was an odd 2-4-4-2 turned out by Baldwin in 1909 and purchased by the Columbia River Belt Line, a Whitney Company operation at Blind Slough on the Lower Columbia. Whitney was one of the few companies that gave names to their engines, instead of numbers. This particular lokey was named the "Skookum." She operated along the river for many years, finally ending her days as Deep River Logging Company's No. 7. She worked steadily until she was wrecked in 1955, just before the end of the Deep River operation. However, she was not badly damaged and she has since been salvaged and hauled away to Seattle to be preserved in a private museum.

First of the more popular 2-6-6-2 tank Mallets was turned out in 1910 for Booth Kelly Lumber Company of Springfield, Oregon. She was delivered as a woodburner, although she was shortly converted to oil. This and a sister engine of much later vintage operated out of Wendling for many years.

After the First World War, Baldwin refined the 2-6-6-2T type, and a good many of them were sold to western loggers. This was a distinct logging type found only in the western woods. Most of them were compounds designed for slow work on heavy grades, but four simple articulated tank engines were built for Weyerhaeuser. During this period, also, the larger, tender-type Mallet was finding favor with Weyerhaeuser and other large operators. The little tank Mallets with their 44-inch drivers had a tractive effort of about 45,000 pounds. The tender type, on the other hand, was designed for mainline service with 51-inch drivers, and being a much larger engine, had a tractive effort of 60,000 pounds.

In 1929 the ultimate in logging locomotives was reached when Baldwin delivered the 200 to Weyerhaeuser. This giant had a 2-8-8-2 wheel arrangement and tipped the scales at more than 355,000 pounds. With her 51-inch drivers she had a tractive effort of 75,000 pounds. In 1933 Baldwin turned out the 201, a sister engine. These were the largest locomotives ever built for a logging railroad. They operated on the line of the Columbia and Cowlitz, out of Longview, Washington, and they normally handled about 90 cars of logs. This train was established by the limitations imposed on returning empties by a 3.7 per cent grade. Forty five cars was the limit, and a ninety car train was doubled over the hill on the return. However, if the occasion required it, they could handle over a hundred cars of logs without difficulty.

Below: Harbor Plywood No. 802, a 2-8-2T, works a cut of cars down to the Milwaukee interchange from the reload at National, Washington.

Albert Farrow

Above: Number 11, of the Coos Bay Lumber Company, busy switching at Powers, Oregon. She was one of several engines of this type owned by Coos Bay. The 11 was slightly smaller than some of them and was used in the woods, while the others saw service over Southern Pacific rails into Marshfield, now Coos Bay.

B. H. Ward

Below: Baldwin 2-6-2 side tanker on the lines of the Ostrander Railway and Timber Company at Ostrander, Washington.

J. M. McClelland, Jr.

Above: Oregon-American No. 104 got away on a spur above Camp Olson and three men were killed: the engineer, fireman and a timekeeper who was hitching a ride. The train had stopped for a section gang on a steep grade, and when they started up too many brakes were released. She was gone before they could catch her again.

A. H. Sliffe

Below: This is how No. 104 looked when they had her back on her feet again. That was back in 1948. No. 104 is still around, the property of a railfan who saved her from the scrappers. At the time of the wreck she was painted a bright green.

A. H. Sliffe

Above: In trouble again. Fresh from the SP&S shops after her big wreck, No. 104 is back in the ditch. Double heading with a plow on her nose, she found a switch frog that was filled with ice.

A. H. Sliffe

Below: Engineer Arlie Sliffe and No. 104 wait for clearance at Keasey.

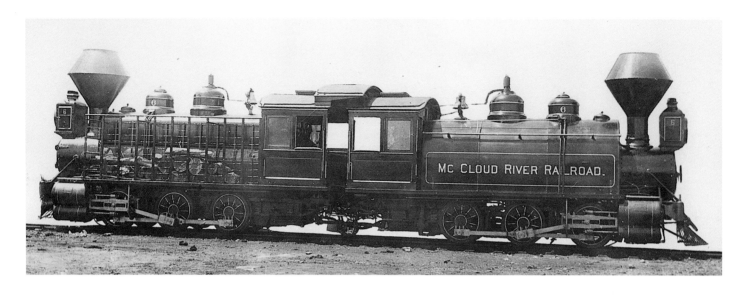

Above: McCloud River's No. 6 was an odd twin—two locomotives joined together. It was soon separated and the two units became individual engines.

B. H. Ward

Below: Deep River Logging Company engine No. 65. This chunky 2-6-2 was built by the American Locomotive Works for B-W Logging Company of Jewell. She was cut up at Deep River when the job ended.

S. B. Lawrence

Above: A Baldwin 2-6-2, of the E. H. Hines Lumber Company, of Westfir, Oregon, is headed for the mill just beyond the bridge. And up above a cab-in-front Mallet of the Southern Pacific is headed for Oakridge and the spectacular climb over the Oregon Cascades.

B. H. Ward

Below: Long-Bell No. 105 pauses at Keasey for water. Despite the new lettering, the operation was forever known as Oregon-American. Long-Bell took over the operations in 1953.

Above: This well-traveled Mike was built by Baldwin in 1910 for the Marysville and Northern, a logging road in northwest Washington. She later came to the Newaukum Valley, at Onalaska, as their No. 901. Carlisle took her over here for a time, and then she was sold to the Valley and Siletz, out of Independence, Oregon. She was finally replaced with a diesel and sent to Portland for scrapping in December 1955.
George B. Abdill

Below: The shop crew admires the new engine just arrived for Smith Powers Lumber Company. No. 101 and her sister, No. 102, were used as road engines between Powers and Coos Bay. They arrived as coal burners, but were soon converted to oil.
John and George Powers

Top: Wisconsin Logging and Timber Company used this little Baldwin to handle the trains between the camp and the dump. No. 7 was inherited from Benson when Wisconsin bought the operation. A sister engine, No. 8, went with Benson across the river to Clatskanie. Second from the left is engineer Jess Bennett. The boy is Arthur Clarkson who grew up to work in engine cabs along the river in later years.
Arthur Clarkson

Middle: Eastern and Western Lumber Company's No. 2, a fat boilered little Prairie, in service at Eufaula. Engineer Charlie Darling stands beside the driver.
Mrs. Becker

Bottom: Silver Falls No. 102 at the mill in Silverton when she was brand new.
Drake photo from A. H. Sliffe

Top: Brooks-Scanlan lost this one on the line south of Bend. The air pump on the 4-spot quit, and when the air was exhausted, she got away. The crew joined the birds and escaped unhurt, except for the fireman. He was still trying to get the pump going when the engine tipped over on him.

Jack Holst

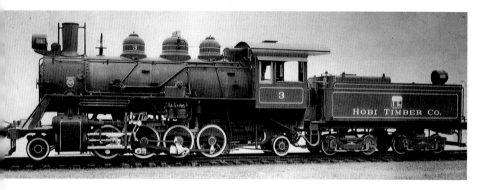

Middle: Baldwin No. 58678, built in September 1925, is typical of the little Mikes that were so popular with loggers in the Twenties. This one was built for service on Grays Harbor.

Courtesy Miller-Freeman Publications

Bottom: Georgia Pacific's No. 1 came to them with the C. D. Johnson lumber Company, of Toledo, Oregon. She is shown here outside the shops at Siletz near the end of her career. With the end of the railroad, she was put on display in Toledo.

Top: Polson Logging Company bought No. 45 as a woodburner back in 1906. She was still hard at work under Rayonier ownership in 1955, but has since been retired. She will be preserved.

Middle: Porter built this trim little Mike in 1927. She came to Crown-Willamette Paper Company from Inman-Poulson Lumber Company in 1936 and was scrapped at Cathlamet in 1959 after having stood idle for many years.

Mrs. Albert Nelson

Bottom: This big Mike carried No. 17 on the Portland and Southwestern Railroad out of Scappoose, Oregon. This was the line of the Clark and Wilson Lumber Company, of Portland.

C. Kinsey photo—Labbe and Goe Collection

Above: A Shelvin-Hixon train at Chemult, Oregon, waits for clearance over the Great Northern rails into Bend. Number 5 was one of several fine Mikes used by this company on its extensive lines southeast of Bend.

B. H. Ward

Below: White River Lumber Company Mike No. 5 dumping logs at the millpond, near Enumclaw, Washington, in the summer of 1945.

Arthur Farrow

Above: The Whitney Company's "Big Jack" brings a train of logs out of the hills along the Kilches River. She is headed for the mill at Garibaldi, Oregon, on Tillamook Bay. Baldwin built her in March of 1920 and she was picked up new by Whitney. They put her to work on Blind Slough on the Columbia, but she went through the track and was shifted to Garibaldi. She didn't fare much better here, and was soon sold to the Tidewater Pacific at Jewell, where she carried No. 53, and where she also served the Astoria Southern. Finally she was sold to the Cowlitz, Chehalis and Cascade, at Chehalis, where she was given No. 25. Today she stands on display in a park in Centralia. Crew cars were often carried next to the engine, as here, to guard against trouble from falling logs or spilled loads.

G. B. Abdill

Below: A Silver Falls Timber Company train arriving at the mill in Silverton. The little Climax on the right poses an interesting question. She is lettered for the Beaver Logging Company, which was miles away at Quincy on the lower Columbia. Beaver had three Climaxes, but none of them were sold to users in the Silverton area.

Oregon Historical Society

Above: Booth-Kelly Lumber Company, of Eugene, was the first to buy a tank Mallet for logging. The engine was turned out by Baldwin in 1910 as a wood burner, but she was soon converted to oil.

Below: Baldwin tank Mallet, as built for Weyerhaeuser Timber Company. These little compound articulateds were found only in the woods of the Northwest. Only about 27 of these engines were built, and four of them were built as simple articulateds.

Miller-Freeman Publications

Above: The "Skookum" made a good name for herself at Blind Slough, just up the river from Astoria. The Columbia River Belt Line was a Whitney Company operation, and in its Centennial Edition of August 1, 1911, the Morning Astorian had the following to say about the Skookum: "The locomotive is an oil burner; total weight of the engine and tender 121½ tons, 65 tons on the drivers, and is especially adapted for a road engine. This locomotive has proven very satisfactory having been in service continually for one year, and during this interval never has caused any delay to the logging operation even though it negotiated, at a maximum, 26 degree curves and 8 per cent grades for three months."

B. H. Ward

Below: When she had finished her job on Blind Slough for the Whitney Company and Larkin and Green, she was sold to the Carlisle Lumber Company of Onalaska, Washington, where she was given No. 7 to replace the name, Skookum.

Lamar Ferguson

Above: Ultimately, the job at Carlisle Lumber Company was finished and the engine was sold again. She was first sent to Mud Bay Logging Company near Olympia, but she didn't work out for them and was returned. She was then sold to Deep River Logging Company, at Deep River, Washington. She was Baldwin No. 33466, built in 1910. Actually, she was turned out by Baldwin as Little River Railroad No. 126, for a company in the East, but she was too much engine for the job and Baldwin resold her to The Whitney Company and a long career in the western woods.
C. W. Mendenhall

Below: Deep River Logging Company dump at Deep River, Washington, as No. 7 comes in with a train.
Albert Farrow

Above: Deep River No. 7 as she looked on an August afternoon in 1955. Backing up to camp with a string of empties, the tank was derailed, and while the crew stood around and contemplated the situation she heaved a sigh and toppled over. Shortly after the picture was taken the scrappers came along and pulled up the rails, leaving her stranded. Five years later she was salvaged for display in a railroad museum near Seattle.

Below: Saginaw Logging Company's No. 4 differed from most tank Mallets in that she had a full saddle tank. On the other engines, the tanks were split and the domes were mounted directly on the boiler.
B. H. Ward

Left: Crown-Zellerbach No. 12. This little tank Mallet was delivered to Crown-Willamette Paper Company in 1929. She and her sister, No. 16, were the last logging engines on the Lower Columbia. They were cut up in 1959. Here she is switching the reload above Cathlamet.

Below: Weyerhauser Mallet No. 120. Baldwin built her in 1936 and Weyerhaeuser put her to work on the line of the Columbia and Cowlitz out of Longview, Washington. She is still hard at work on Grays Harbor as Rayonier's No. 120.

C. Kinsey photo from Cecil Davis

Above: Weyerhaeuser Timber Company No. 201 at Headquarters Camp, above Longview. This and No. 200, a sister engine, were the largest locomotives ever built for logging railroads. They handled 90 cars of logs with ease, limited only by the 3.7 per cent grade which cut them down to 45 empties on the return trip, which meant doubling the train back up the hill. They doubled this train over the hill.

D. S. Richter

Below: Long-Bell Mallet was used at Ryderwood, and over the Longview, Portland and Northern line of Long-Bell into Longview, Washington. She was Baldwin No. 57597, one of a pair delivered in 1924.

Wilson photo from J. M. McClelland, Jr.

Above: Weyerhaeuser No. 112 is typical of many tank Mallets turned out by Baldwin for W.T. Co. in the twenties and thirties. No. 112 was one of the last of them, having been built in 1937. She was later sold to Kosmos Timber Company as their No. 12 and then to U.S. Plywood Corporation. When she was scrapped at Amboy, Washington in late 1959 she was the property of International Paper Company—and she carried the name of Harbor Plywood on her tank and No. 12 on her cab. Her history was typical of many of the engines that were built for use in the woods.

West Coast Lumbermen's Association

Above: Harbor Plywood No. 12 delivers a train of logs to the Northern Pacific at Yacolt, Washington, in 1957. It wasn't long after International Paper Company took over the operation that they also acquired the Northern Pacific branch into Vancouver.

Albert Farrow

Below: A Long-Bell Mallet thunders across a trestle near Ryderwood, Washington, in August of 1950, shortly before the job ended.

Albert Farrow

Left: Red River Lumber Company train during a layover in Chester, California. This was possibly the only logging railroad to use electric motors on their trains. The locomotives were operated on 1500 volt DC current picked up from a wire that hung to the side of the right of way to provide clearance for the log loads. Note the odd trolley designed to swing out to the side for the pickup. Red River also used a gas-electric locomotive long before this type of engine came into general favor.

B. H. Ward

Below: Weyerhaeuser No. 201 drifts across the Cowlitz River bridge, near Longview, with a train of loaded skeleton cars.

Weyerhaeuser Company

Left: Weyerhaeuser Timber Company's No. 120 heads down from the woods with twenty loads.

C. Kinsey photo from Cecil Davis

Below: Simpson Logging Company train on the line out of Shelton, Washington. The tank Mallet carries No. 13, a number rarely found on woods engines.

Chet Ullin photo from West Coast Lumbermen's Association

Above: Long-Bell's Willamette engine No. 106 on a stretch of heavy grade above Keasey, Oregon.

End of the Show

The end came on an August day in 1957. The Long-Bell division of International Paper Company finished logging in the hills overlooking Keasey, Oregon, and it was over. The era of the railroad logging show was history. It didn't take very long, really. There are men alive today whose memories cover it all—from the bull teams to the present.

Oh sure, logging railroads are still serving the West from California to British Columbia. Some of them are still steam; and if you know where to go, you can still hear the song of the Shay. But it's not the same. The logs come down to the reload from the spar tree on big diesel trucks, and the loads are swung from the trucks to the railroad cars in a single operation. The railroad takes them from the reload to the dump. This is short line railroading.

Up at Keasey they logged with the railroad. The railroad was laid right up to the landing, and then an old tree rigged skidder was nudged up to the spar tree. And when the black smoke smudged the sky and the steam roared from the exhausts the logs came singing in along the skyline.

They laid the rail to the spar tree. And when the side was logged they pulled the rail up and laid it down again in a new spot. But the skidder side wasn't the only one. There were other sides, and one of them was a steam side, with a steam yarder bringing in the logs and a steam loader handling the boom. It kept the section crews busy pulling up the rail and laying it down again. And when they moved the steam sides they moved the hundreds of feet of pipeline that carried the water to the donkeys. It lay on the ties beside the rail. And they slid the watchman's shanty onto the moving car and took it along, too. The watchman lived alone in the woods beside the track to watch for fire, and to get up steam in the early morning and keep an eye on the water pump. If you liked seclusion and a little fresh venison now and then, this could be a fine job.

This was the old Oregon-American Lumber Company. They came to Vernonia in 1922, and they started out with all the best equipment that money could buy. Everything was brand new. And in 1957 a lot of that equipment was still in use. For 35 years they kept the big mill in Vernonia humming. They logged all the way up Rock Creek, and they worked their way south to the edge of the Salmonberry. They took in parts of Tillamook and Clatsop and Columbia Counties, and when they finished they were right back where they started. You could stand at the landing on the steam side and look down on the little station at Keasey, far below.

So the day came when there was no more timber to cut. There was no place left to lay the rails. They loaded out the equipment and they picked up their tools and left. The steam pots were cut up where they stood.

Left: A graphic illustration of the voracious appetite of the steam skidder. They have marched across the landscape laying waste to hundreds of acres of virgin timber. The top quality logs have been harvested, and everything else has been trampled underfoot, leaving a fertile field for fire. And the fire came during the great Tillamook Burn. This was at the edge of the great burn, but much of what is shown here was burned. Today these logging methods are as obsolete as the equipment that made them possible.

C. Kinsey photo from Ed Peterson

Below: Fire has always been the greatest menace faced by loggers. This railroad trestle was consumed in the fire that marked the end of the Silver Falls Timber Company operation at Silverton.

Drake photo from the Oregon Historical Society

Above: Trim little Prairie engine assigned to mainline duties between Vernonia and the camps. Here she is bringing the machinery down from the woods at the end of operations, backing down the spur to the mill in Vernonia. She has been saved by a fan who hopes to preserve her.

Gregory Kamholz

Below: Long-Bell No. 106, a Willamette engine, waits at the skidder for the crew at quitting time. This old tree-rigged machine was probably the last skidder in service on the west coast. A month after this picture was taken, railroad logging was a thing of the past.

Above: Deep River No. 65, a little 2-6-2, rumbles across Salmon Creek trestle on an August day in 1955. Just behind the tank is the tiny crummy built on a single disconnected truck. Not long after, No. 65 made the last trip for Deep River.

Below: Silver Falls Timber Company Mike pulls into Silverton with a train of logs. This is believed to be the last train of logs to be taken out by Silver Falls in 1936, after which the line was pulled up.

Drake photo from the Oregon Historical Society

Above: Long-Bell No. 103, a big Lima Shay, crosses highway No. 26 on her way down from Camp Olson. She is heading for Camp McGregor, where she will turn her train over to a rod engine for the haul into Vernonia. Crew cars between the camp and the woods make a stop here to pick up the men who live outside of camp.

Gregory Kamholz

Below: St. Regis Paper Company Heisler No. 91 working the dump at Mineral Lake, Washington, back in September 1953.

Albert Farrow

Above: Rayonier No. 3 has just been restored for display in Promised Land Park along Highway 101. To prove she still had life in her, she was fired up and put through her paces.

Opposite page: Spectacular bridge near Mayfield, Washington, on the Cowlitz, Chehalis and Cascade Railway. This short line was built to serve the logging industry. It ended operations in May 1955 when the Long-Bell camp near Mayfield was closed. In the photo, No. 20, an ex-Northern Pacific 4-8-0, makes the last trip over the bridge. The bridge was condemned near the last and two engines were used. One pushed the train across, after which the crew walked across and continued on the other side.

Below: A Rayonier train pauses at a junction near Sappho. The carefully maintained lokey is the last engine turned out by the Willamette Iron and Steel Company. She was sold to J. Neils, of Klickitat, in December 1929, but was later sold and put to work up on the Olympic Peninsula.

Bert Ward

Left: Crown-Zellerbach tower skidder shortly before it was scrapped at Cathlamet. This was the Willamette machine.

Below: Climax No. 4 of the Eagle Gorge Logging Railway backing down with a train near Eagle Gorge, Washington, in September 1955. This was the last true railroad logging show in the state of Washington.

Alber Farrow

Above: Georgia Pacific No. 9 headed for the reload with a string of empties a month before the end. When G-P pulled the fire on the 9-spot on the last day of 1959, it marked more than the end of the railroad. It was also the very end of the disconnected truck. But not of the little tank engine. MGM bought her to use in wreck scenes of a movie.

Below: Crown-Zellerbach No. 6. She is Willamette engine No. 13, delivered to Crown-Willamette Paper Company at Astoria in January 1924. Later transferred to Cathlamet, the 6-spot was still serviceable when the line was pulled up in 1955. She is now on display alongside the Cathlamet office.

Above: Beautiful Vance Creek bridge on the Simpson Company's line out of Shelton, Washington. Simpson has a number of these fine bridges.

Forde & Carter photo from West Coast Lumbermen's Assoociation

Above: Kosmos Timber Company No. 10 heads out of the woods near Kosmos, Washington, with a train for the Milwaukee interchange. A Heisler waits in the hole to give her a hand up the hill.

Alber Farrow

Below: Big Pacific Coast Shay still at work out of Klickitat, Washington. She is No. 7 of the J. Neils Lumber Company operation, now St. Regis Paper Company.

Jack Holst

Above: West Side Shay No. 14 heads out over the graceful curve of Niagara Creek bridge.

Both pictures: John S. Anderson

Opposite page: Almost an anachronism in this day and age is the busy operation of the West Side Lumber Company, of Tuolumne, California. More than 60 miles of three-foot gauge track extends back into the mountains from the mill, and the trains are handled by big, three-truck Lima Shays. Here we see No. 14 getting up steam for the 2:00 A.M. run out of Camp 45 on a June night in 1958.

Above: West Side Shay No. 14 passes the site of old Camp 21 on her way down to Tuolumne, with an oil car and reefer on ahead of the loads. Just to her right is a drop of over a thousand feet to the Clavey River.

John S. Anderson

Right: McCloud River Railroad, back in the days of steam. Here, 2-8-2 No. 26 handles a log train at Bartle, California.

B. H. Ward

Below: Rayonier No. 38 on her way to the dump near Hoquiam in August of 1959. Built by Baldwin for Weyerhaeuser in 1934, she became their No. 4 on the line out of Klamath Falls, but she gained greater fame as the Sierra Railroad No. 38. She is still hard at work for Rayonier.

Albert Farrow

Above: Rayonier No. 90 crossing Prairie River trestle on an August day in 1959. This spotless little Mike is still hard at work on the Grays Harbor operation.

Albert Farrow

Below: Rayonier's No. 120 darkens the spring sky as she works a train down to the dump on the Hoquiam River. Baldwin turned out No. 120 for Weyerhaeuser in 1937. Photo was taken April 20, 1959.

Albert Farrow

Right: After the loggers have gone! Silver Falls Timber Company logged this area, after which it burned. The scene looks blighted and desolate—but the brush and grass have started to cover the ground, and before many years it will be green again.

June Drake from the Oregon Historical Society

Below: West Side Shay No. 9 on River Bridge across the North Fork of the Tuolumne River late on an October afternoon in 1959. River Bridge is well known for the unusual straight section with curved approaches.

John S. Anderson

Above: The last train long ago rumbled out of Camp Neverstill, crossed the Nehalem River and made its slow way up through the tunnel on the way to Kerry. And now, except for the sighing of the wind and the croaking of the frogs, Neverstill is still at last.

Glossary

"A" frame: A frame of logs or timbers in the shape of a capital A, used for lifting by means of a cable passing through a block at the peak of the frame.

articulated locomotive: One that is built over two separate sets of engines, the first of which is free to swing beneath the locomotive frame, giving the unit great flexibility on sharp curves.

block: Steel frame with hook or eye attached enclosing a pulley wheel, used for guiding the line.

boom: Area in the water where logs are stored. Also the frame carrying the rigging used in loading.

boomer: Term borrowed from railroaders to denote men on the railroad crews who changed jobs often. Also the common designation for the mountain beaver.

brow log: A large log laid beside the track at the dump or landing to prevent logs swinging against the cars.

bullcook: The kitchen helper and general handyman around camp. The term was also used by loggers to identify the engines assigned to work train service.

bunk: Or log bunk. The bolster on cars or trucks that carried the log.

bunkhouse: Sleeping quarters for the single men.

camp: Woods site of the company's shops, offices, living quarters, etc.

camp car: A building on railroad trucks. These cars were often grouped together to make up a camp, which in turn could be moved as the operation progressed.

cant: A large sawn timber intended for resawing into smaller dimensions. Also to turn a log. Also to make lean.

cheese blocks: Wedge-shaped block, or chock, carried in the log bunk to hold the logs in place.

cold deck: A pile of logs held in temporary storage, whether in the woods or at the mill.

compound locomotive: One that uses steam exhausted from one cylinder, or set of cylinders, to operate a second cylinder, or set of cylinders.

crew car: Any car used to carry the crew to work in the woods.

crummy: A term borrowed from railroaders to designate the caboose, if one was used. Also applied to the crew car.

crotchline: A method of loading using two tongs hung from a spreader bar. The spreader bar was hung between the mainline and the haulback and could be swung back and forth, or raised and lowered by manipulating the drums controlling the two lines.

disconnects: Four-wheel trucks with couplers on both ends used for hauling logs. Logs resting across two trucks made up a car, which was held together by the weight of the load.

dogs: Metal pins, or hooks, having an eye in one end. These were driven into a log so that several could be fastened together with chain or cable. Used for dragging logs along a skidroad or for movement in water.

donkey: A self-powered winch used for pulling logs in from the woods, loading, etc. Originally steam powered with a vertical boiler mounted, with the drums, on a sled made from logs.

donkey doctor: The machinist who repaired and maintained the donkey engines.

donkey engine: *see donkey.*

donkey puncher: The engineer who operated the donkey.

double: As to "double a train." A railroad term used to describe the operation whereby a train was separated and taken up a grade a section at a time.

drum: The spool of the winch on a donkey engine around which the line was wound.

dummy: An early steam motor designed for use in city streets and having a superstructure resembling a coach.

dump: The point at which the logs were unloaded from the cars, usually a boom or millpond.

endhooks: Used for picking up logs in loading. They were an L shaped piece of iron having an eye for the line in one end and a barb to dig into the log at the other.

flats: Or log flats. Flatcars used for hauling logs and equipped with bunks.

friction: The clutch by which the donkey drums were engaged.

geared engine: Any locomotive in which the power from the cylinders was transmitted to the wheels through gears.

gillpoke: *see jillpoke.*

gypsy drum: A small drum, usually mounted on an extension of one of the shafts of a donkey and not capable of being disengaged. Early donkeys did most of their work with such drums, but on later donkeys it was used mostly for handling the strawline.

haulback: A lighter line attached to the mainline for returning the rigging to the woods. Also used to identify other equipment used with it, such as the haulback drum and the haulback block.

hayrack: A type of loading boom, rectangular in shape, and hung from the spar tree so that the side pieces straddle the tree to hold it in place. Two lines are used in loading with this boom, a tong being hung from each; and they are so positioned on the boom that they are in line with the car when the boom is swung over it.

heelboom: A type of loading boom using but one tong. The tong is hung on the log back of the point of balance. When the log is raised the back end comes up first and "heels" against the boom, forcing the other end to raise. The latest refinement in loading, as it kept the logs from swinging as they were handled.

hickey: A metal handle used by the brakemen in setting up the hand brakes.

hog: A railroad term to indicate an engine.

hole: Used by the brakemen to indicate the area between the loads where they stood to apply the brakes.

incline: A cable-operated railroad going straight up the side of a hill.

jillpoke: A rod, or pole, used as a lever to prevent movement in one direction, as a prop. Also any such lever, or prop, inadvertently interfering with movement.

lead: A block, or roller, designed to lead a cable into a specific position. Also used to indicate the position, as "to give it the proper lead."

landing: The area where logs from the woods are gathered for loading aboard transportation.

leverman: The engineer who controls the operation of a skidder. Similar to the puncher on a donkey.

line: Any of the ropes or cables used in the woods. Also the boundary lines, or survey lines.

load: A loaded car.

loader: The man who loads the cars. He must choose the logs to make a load and see that they are loaded securely. Railroad operations usually used a head loader and a second loader. Also the donkey used in loading.

log bunk: *see bunk.*

lokey: Also lokie. Common term used in the woods for locomotive.

mainline: The main line on a donkey, which is used for the heavy pull. Also used to denote the main railroad line; the permanent line from which the spurs radiate.

mallet: Pronounced mal-lee. A compound articulated locomotive, named for the designer. Often improperly applied to any articulated locomotive.

mikado: Or Mike. An engine having a 2-8-2 wheel arrangement.

millpond: The pond in which the logs for the mill are contained, whether it be an artificial pond or a boom within an existing body of water. Usually referred to as the pond.

mogul: An engine having a 2-6-0 wheel arrangement.

moving car: Specially designed heavy duty flatcar used for moving donkeys, camp buildings, tractors and other heavy equipment.

mulligan car: The crew car. Sometimes used in early days for carrying hot meals (mulligan) to the woods crews at noon.

old growth: First growth, or virgin timber. Growing slowly for centuries, this timber usually attained a size and fineness of texture not found in newer timber.

operation: The woods plant of a logging company.

operator: The owner, or contractor, of a logging operation.

parbuckle: To roll a log by running a cable under it and back over the top. By pulling the top line the log was rolled forward. Often used in loading from a rollway.

peavey: A tool composed of a long straight handle with a steel point on one end and a hook hinged near the point. The hook was sunk into a log and the handle used to exert leverage to turn the log. Next to the saw and ax, the most useful tool in the woods.

pole road: A railroad made of small poles in lieu of rails.

pot: Or steam pot. A steam donkey.

prairie: A locomotive having a 2-6-2 wheel arrangement.

puncher: *see donkey puncher.*

punk: *see whistle punk.*

punking whistles: The act of sending instructions to the donkey puncher on the whistle wire. This was done by sending impulses in the form of waves along the taut wire. When the waves reached the donkey, they gave a short tug on the whistle lever. Complicated whistle combinations could be sent in quick succession by a good whistle punk—and they had better be right!

railroad logging: Used to denote the type of logging operation in which the railroad went right out to the spar tree in the woods and picked up the logs directly from the yarder.

reload: A point at which logs are transferred from one carrier to another, as from trucks to railroad cars.

rigging: The combination of blocks and line used in the woods, as the rigging in a spar tree. Also the act of setting it up.

road engine: The locomotive used on the mainline to handle the loads brought out of the spurs by other engines. Also used in early days to denote the donkey that skidded logs from the yarder to the landing, sometimes for great distances.

rod engine: Standard locomotive in which the power is transmitted to the wheels from the cylinders by a mainrod and siderods.

rollway: A sloping deck of poles or logs, usually at a landing, for storing logs. Logs were rolled aboard the cars by hand and by gravity. Parbuckling from a rollway was the first application of power to the loading operation.

rooster: A metal bar, or spacer, used to couple disconnected trucks when it was impractical to bring them close enough together to use the regular coupler.

saddletank: A locomotive on which the water tank was carried over the boiler.

schoolmarm: A tree with a divided trunk. Two trees growing from a single stump.

second growth: Young growth timber.

sets: Disconnected trucks were usually made up of a matched pair. Footboards and brakes were on opposite ends so that when made into a car, brakes would be on the same side of the train and footboards were at each end of the car. Thus, two trucks made a set.

sheave: Usually pronounced shiv. The grooved wheel in a block that carried the line.

show: Used to indicate the immediate area of operation. Also the type of logging, such as donkey show, caterpillar show, etc.

side: The operation revolving around one landing. An operation could be made up of several sides.

side tank: A tank engine on which the tanks were carried on either side of the boiler.

simple locomotive: An articulated locomotive in which all of the cylinders receive steam directly from the boiler.

skeleton car: Also called connected trucks. A car in which the trucks are held together by a center beam, but having no deck. Such cars made air brakes possible throughout the train.

skidder: A logging machine combining yarder and loader, and mounted on railroad trucks. There were two types: tree rigged, which made use of a regular spar tree; and tower skidders, which carried a steel tower in lieu of a spar tree.

skid road: The path along which logs are dragged to the spar tree. Also the roads used by the early ox and horse teams for skidding logs.

skyline: A heavy line, sometimes of great length, strung between two points, along which ran a carriage rigged for carrying logs. There were various designs, but their purpose was to carry logs above the ground to avoid difficult terrain, or to span gullies, etc.

snipe: A beveled edge chopped around the end of a log to prevent its catching as it was skidded. Also the act of cutting the beveled edge.

spar tree: A tree from which the top and limbs have been trimmed, used to hang rigging for logging. Usually a tree was chosen where it grew, but if none was available, one might be brought in and raised for the purpose.

speeder: Gasoline or diesel cars ranging in use from those of the section gang to those used for transporting the crew back and forth from the woods. The latter were usually called crew speeders.

spool: To wind line around a donkey drum.

spool donkey: One of the earliest types, using a vertical capstan, rather than a drum.

spot: Used in conjunction with the locomotive number in common parlance. Most woods engines carried low numbers and were referred to as the 2-spot, 5-spot, 10-spot, etc.

steam motor: Correct designation for the steam dummy.

steam pot: Steam donkey.

stick: Slang term for a log or tree.

strap: Short piece of line with an eye spliced in both ends.

strawline: A light line used for odd jobs, such as pulling heavier line into place. Often used with the gypsy drum, although later donkeys incorporated a strawline drum. Commonly referred to as the "haywire."

swing: Used to denote the operation when a donkey was interposed between the yarder and the landing. This was the swing donkey. It swung the logs from the yarder to the loader.

tailblock: The farthest block from the donkey around which the line reversed its direction of travel.

tailhold: The point where the end of a line was fastened in a fixed position, as to a stump.

tank engine: A locomotive in which the water and fuel tanks were carried over the drivers, instead of in a tender.

tram road: In railroad usage it usually indicated a road made from sawn timbers, rather than steel rails. Sometimes used to denote a pole road.

turn: The logs brought out of the woods in a single pull, whether it be the turn handled by a donkey, tractor, truck or train.

whistle punk: The individual who relayed the signals from the woods crew to the donkey puncher. Usually the starting job for beginners in the woods. *See punking whistles.*

widowmaker: A falling limb, or other debris, that might bring instant oblivion to the unwary logger.

yarder: The donkey engaged in bringing logs to the spar tree from the point where they were cut.

Index